THE SLOW LANE

Why Quick Fixes Fail and How to Achieve Real Change

SASCHA HASELMAYER

BK

Berrett–Koehler Publishers, Inc.

Berrett-Koehler Publishers, Inc.
1333 Broadway, Suite 1000
Oakland, CA 94612-1921
Tel: (510) 817-2277
Fax: (510) 817-2278
www.bkconnection.com

ORDERING INFORMATION

Quantity sales. Special discounts are available on quantity purchases by corporations, associations, and others. For details, contact the "Special Sales Department" at the Berrett-Koehler address above.

Individual sales. Berrett-Koehler publications are available through most bookstores. They can also be ordered directly from Berrett-Koehler: Tel: (800) 929-2929; Fax: (802) 864-7626; www.bkconnection.com.

Orders for college textbook / course adoption use. Please contact Berrett-Koehler: Tel: (800) 929-2929; Fax: (802) 864-7626.

Distributed to the U.S. trade and internationally by Penguin Random House Publisher Services.

Berrett-Koehler and the BK logo are registered trademarks of Berrett-Koehler Publishers, Inc.

Printed in Canada

Berrett-Koehler books are printed on long-lasting acid-free paper. When it is available, we choose paper that has been manufactured by environmentally responsible processes. These may include using trees grown in sustainable forests, incorporating recycled paper, minimizing chlorine in bleaching, or recycling the energy produced at the paper mill.

Library of Congress Cataloging-in-Publication Data
    Names: Haselmayer, Sascha, author.
    Title: The slow lane : why quick fixes fail and how to achieve real change / Sascha Haselmayer.
    Description: First edition. | Oakland, CA : Berrett-Koehler Publishers, [2023] | Includes bibliographical references and index.
    Identifiers: LCCN 2022058284 (print) | LCCN 2022058285 (ebook) | ISBN 9781523004584 (paperback) | ISBN 9781523004591 (pdf) | ISBN 9781523004607 (epub) | ISBN 9781523004614 (audio)
    Subjects: LCSH: Social change. | Organizational change. | Problem solving. | Social problems.
    Classification: LCC HM831 .H287 2023 (print) | LCC HM831 (ebook) | DDC 303.4—dc23/eng/20230206
    LC record available at https://lccn.loc.gov/2022058284
    LC ebook record available at https://lccn.loc.gov/2022058285

First Edition

30 29 28 27 26 25 24 23 | 10 9 8 7 6 5 4 3 2 1

Book producer and text designer: BookMatters
Cover designer: Frances Baca

To Julia, Sofía, Olivia, Currito, and Mochi

Contents

Foreword

In 2021, Sascha Haselmayer wrote a piece for *The Commons* in which he noted that "shared public bicycles—first invented by citizens of Amsterdam in 1965—took more than thirty years to catch on."[1] The year 1998 saw the first technologically enabled city bike-share program, but six years later, in 2004, only thirteen cities had jumped on the bandwagon. By 2010 that number had swelled to four hundred, but it took another decade for shared bicycles, and now scooters, to become as ubiquitous as sidewalks.

The piece was called "Fast Tech, Slow Change."[2] Sascha's point was that public innovations take a *long* time, typically forty years, to take off at a scale that changes people's lives. His bike-share example stuck in my mind; I have used it often in my work at New America when it seems like deep electoral reform will never happen, an infrastructure of care will never be built, we will never invest properly in early education and overhaul pre-K–12 and higher education, and an equal society that meets people where they are is a pipedream. It is a gospel of hope for people who work for fundamental change to improve the quality of people's lives.

This book explores and distills the design principles that

enable slow change to happen, in many different contexts and at many different levels. From the family dinner table to the Icelandic banking crisis, these Slow Lane Principles can enable inclusive, deliberative, creative, lasting change. Time is not the enemy but an ally, at least up the point that slow change is lasting change.

Most important, the Slow Lane process decouples speed from scale. Fast Lane processes strip away complexity in favor of focus, circumventing what Sascha calls "the human mess" of conflicting desires and emotions to instead deliver measurable outputs. "Move fast and break things" is the now discredited mantra of Silicon Valley; indeed, the definition of "disruption" is a sharp break in the status quo. Fast, furious, and focused has been seen as the key to disrupting entire systems—of transport, commerce, communications, education, and many other systems—and thereby achieving change at systemic scale.

Slow Lane change is no less wedded to scale. Social entrepreneurs also seek to change entire systems. Many public problem solvers focus on changing government policies and the implementation of those policies precisely because government works at a scale that even the biggest corporations can rarely achieve. Yet the changemakers featured in the following pages have learned, often the hard way, that speed can be the enemy of scale. Fast solutions often simply don't stick.

The right speed, as this book repeatedly reminds us, is "the speed of trust." Only trust can convince the marginalized and excluded people that changemakers typically seek to "help" to speak up, say what they think, and share what they know. And only knowledge at that granular level can identify the levers that need to be pulled to make tangible change in people's lives. Once trust is built, processes *can* speed up. It is all a matter of sequencing.

Trust must flow both ways in a change process. Individuals trapped in dysfunctional systems must believe in the possibility of real and lasting change. Yet those who would help enable that change must also trust. It turns out that trust on the part of those who hold power means more than believing; it requires sharing agency and relinquishing control. Behavior change that is hard and scary is typically required all around, at every phase of and for every participant in the change process.

A theme running through *The Slow Lane*, wide and deep enough to be a river, is the critical importance of human relationships. As Italian physicist Carlo Rovelli explains, talking about quantum physics, "relationships are the key to existence." He continues: "We understand reality better if we think of it in terms of interactions, not individuals."[3] In the same vein, Sascha explains in "Fast Tech, Slow Change" why his effort to offer municipal procurement software as a service to improve the performance of a large number of cities failed.

> We had also underestimated the benefit of human contact in the process. The richness of our relationships with city employees and the leadership function we held during our consulting work could not be duplicated in a SaaS [Software as a Service] offering.... We didn't realize that our process also featured empathy, encouragement, and human support that helped our clients complete the process. Yes, the tech product we were offering had all the same functions and workflows, but lacked the important intangibles of human contact and relationships.

In sum, change in human behavior requires a particular kind and duration of human connection.

I plan to put the lessons of this book to use immediately, in my personal and professional relations. Perhaps I will be

more effective in bringing about changes I would like to see at
home, in my workplace, or in the work I hope to see done in the
world. Regardless, I will slow down, listen better, share more,
ask open-ended questions, and not expect technological magic.
That's a rich harvest from a little book.

Anne-Marie Slaughter, CEO of New America and
Bert G. Kerstetter '66 University Professor Emerita
of Politics and International Affairs
Princeton University

Preface

We live in a world of quick fixes. In business, government, and society we celebrate the entrepreneurs, hackers, and disruptors who try to deal with change by finding shortcuts. They give us a sense that any big problem can be resolved by a daring, often technological solution. But, as the past decades have repeatedly shown, these quick fixes are nothing more than an illusion. It turns out that there is no technical fix to climate change, injustice, discrimination, pollution, or rising inequality. And yet we continue to glorify leaders who promise to fix things for us. I call this phenomenon the Fast Lane.

In business the Fast Lane gives us companies like Facebook that look past hate speech to gain a dominant position in the market faster. In politics the Fast Lane gives us leaders who assert their "leadership" by imposing quick fixes in moments of crisis, like the austerity measures that threw millions of people into poverty following the global financial crisis of 2007–2008. And at home the Fast Lane poisons our relationships. Parents reduce their children's lives to a race to the top, justifying any means necessary to get their ends. In the Fast Lane leaders at all levels of society adhere to the same playbook: act fast by canceling the voices of others, and exercise power decisively.

But instead of the progress it promises, this behavior fuels a downward spiral of growing inequality and division that leaves our most urgent problems unsolved.

I consider myself to be a product of the Fast Lane. Growing up, my parents defined success in strictly monetary terms as well as by our ability to come out on top of others. Eventually my deep desire for social change led me out of the Fast Lane because it simply wasn't any good at delivering real change. From there I quite literally stumbled into the Slow Lane.

For twenty years I had been a quick-fixer. I traveled the world to help governments and communities solve their problems faster. But wherever I went, the reality on the ground tried to teach me something else entirely. It took a visit to a notorious prison in London in 2014 to open my eyes to what I had seen all along: that the quickest way to change the world is to slow down and listen. Here I was, seeing social change happen right in front of my eyes in the most unlikely of places. It happened because Kevin Reilly, the prison governor, had the humility to not respond to a crisis by trying to fix things quickly. Instead, he had the humility to ask the prisoners to help him solve the prison's problems—something that had not happened in the prison's 172-year lifetime. This simple yet counterintuitive response connected the dots in a new way to what I had seen the world over. The Slow Lane came into focus.

The Slow Lane is at work all around us. Most notably, it is made up of movements for social progress. Such movements have an urgent desire for change, to tackle injustices like the broken probation system in the UK or the chronic levels of homelessness in American cities. Unlike the Fast Lane, however, these movements choose not to cancel out the complicated voices of others to get things done. Instead, they create the kind of trusted conversation that brings people together. This is what seemingly slows these movements down, making it easy to overlook them entirely in a world that celebrates big, decisive action. But this slowness is incredibly productive, as it empowers even the most disadvantaged people to become active contributors to change. Over time, this social capital can lead to the kind of explosive and transformative change that fundamentally replaces a broken system with new laws, mindsets, behaviors, or economies.

Successful Slow Lane movements adhere to five common principles. They need to **hold their urgency (#1)**, accepting the notion that even in moments of crisis they have to move at the speed of trust instead of rushing to action. They're great **listeners (#2)**, acting with humility that builds the kind of trust that opens hearts and minds to transformative new ideas. To do this, Slow Lane movements also **share their agency (#3)**, meaning that they provide pathways for everyone, even the least prepared, to contribute and lead. And contrary to the common perception that inclusive movements are not agile or inventive, Slow Lane movements turn out to **nurture curiosity (#4)** to a very high degree, innovating by seeking inspiration from science, arts, or other movements. This is how they retain the flexibility to adapt creatively to changing circumstances. Successful Slow Lane movements **use technology as an enabler (#5)**, putting it at the service of their mission for social change, and have created a new playbook that withstands the dominance plays of the traditional tech startup playbook.

These insights are valuable not just for people involved in social change. Even in the intimacy of our homes, we are faced with the same daunting challenges. Do we empower our children by extending our trust to them to build their life? Or do we seek comfort in what appears to be the proven playbook of parenthood: pushing them to get ahead of others, playing by the rules of the Fast Lane? Here our trade-offs become much clearer, as we have to navigate the complexity of being trusting

with unconditional love and seeking refuge in becoming the
benign dictators that helicopter their offspring to success in
a Fast Lane world. At home, too, we can choose to adhere to
the Slow Lane Principles. Hold the urgency, listen, share the
agency, and nurture curiosity—these practices will help us not
just empower our children but prepare them for a Slow Lane
world. The Slow Lane, it turns out, offers lessons at any scale:
for me, my family, my work, my community, my movement, my
business, and my government.

This book offers a timely response to our growing sense of
crisis and frustration at our inability to make a difference and
change things. I have written *The Slow Lane* for people who
want to make a difference. They include social entrepreneurs
and people involved in a movement or a community. And, as I
report in Chapter 7, they include the millions of entrepreneurs
who started their business to make a difference. They include
public servants, people in government, or elected officials. And
they include people who care and wish to make a difference at
home, in their families, among their friends, in their communities, or society. *The Slow Lane* offers a holistic alternative,
connecting the dots instead of dividing the world up into single
topics like social innovation, parenting, government innovation,
the ecosystem of philanthropy, activism, or economic inclusion.
It explains how the efforts of millions of people across all these
sectors are coming together. And what our new journey looks
like. Where the Fast Lane has penetrated our families, communities, jobs, economy, and politics, the Slow Lane offers a new
set of mind-sets and practices that help leaders deliver the kind
of change and future we all hope for. Where others tend to pit
sectors of society against one another by vilifying government,
civil society, or business, *The Slow Lane* finds common ground,
starting with the inner work and motivation that help meaningful change come about.

I am fortunate to have lived and worked in these different worlds, thus I am offering to be a guide to the Slow Lane from the inside. As a social entrepreneur, I have built movements and businesses and have worked alongside the world's leading innovators in government, philanthropy, society, and business. I have lived and worked in the communities I write about. And as a citizen and parent, I have grappled to find my role every day. All this gives me firsthand insight that adds nuance to the stories in this book. My stories reveal that you don't have to be a super-human to join the Slow Lane, but that it is made up of people who struggle with the same choices, doubts, and setbacks we all face. I am delighted to share these stories with you and hope that they spark new insights and ideas.

Introduction

Slow Is the New Fast

He who rushes ahead, doesn't go far.

Lao Tzu

I lived in Barcelona when the global financial crisis struck in 2007–2008. For three decades Spain had been a poster child for economic growth and success in Europe. Now the country was hit hard. Like politicians everywhere, Spain's leaders felt compelled to act fast.

The Bitterest Medicine of the Financial Crisis: Our Rush to Action

Overwhelmed by the collapse and complexity of the financial system, Spain's leaders yielded to the pressure and advice of international experts in economics and finance. They concluded that the only way to restore order was to invest billions of euros to bail out the banks that would otherwise put the whole economy at risk. Leaders went on to prescribe what became known as "the bitter medicine": the government would have to implement tough austerity measures, which meant higher taxes and deep cuts to public services, to pay for the bailout. Their goal was to reassure financial markets and the European Union, a big lender, that Spain would continue to pay interest on its mounting debt.

The bitter medicine, a product of the rushed desire to show leadership and quickly return things to normal, brought little relief. Unemployment rose from 8 percent in 2007 to 21 percent by 2011. The number of people living in extreme poverty·tripled in the same period. With every year, millions more people lost their jobs and had to rely on less and less government support. As cuts took hold, education, health, and social services deteriorated. Spain became the country with the highest inequality in Europe. Young people were among those suffering the most, unable to build their lives. When in 2011 youth unemployment topped 50 percent, protests erupted.

One morning in May, as I walked my daughters to school, we stumbled upon a newly erected protest camp in Plaza Catalunya, Barcelona's main commercial square. Two hundred protesters, inspired by the Arab Spring, had put up tents and tree houses overnight. Their occupation of the square, carried out simultaneously by activists in Madrid, had two goals. They wanted to force the government to listen to the people who were hit the hardest by the austerity measures. And they wanted to create a new space for people to meet and develop their own ideas for the future. They called themselves *indignados* (translates as "indignant," "outraged"), and their anger was directed at politicians, officials, experts, and the economy in general.

Frustrated by not being heard, at least seven million Spaniards, about 15 percent of the population, had joined the *indignados* in protests by 2015. At the outset this movement had no clear vision or agenda for the future. It sprang out of a citizenry known for being among the least politically engaged in Europe. But the leaderless movement developed an agenda and grew into a significant political force. In 2015 they swept mayors from established political parties out of four of the five largest cities in local elections. In Barcelona, Ada Colau, an activist and leader of a new political party, Barcelona En Comú, was elected mayor. She rejected the privileges and backroom dealmaking of her predecessors and instead insisted on holding all official meetings in public, on the street. Her message was clear: I am listening to you.

Four years later, in 2019, the general election results in Spain showed just how far the political transformation had gone: the Socialist and Popular parties, who for decades had divided 97 percent of the votes between them, had now lost half their voters to upstarts with roots in the protest movements. When a government was at last formed in 2020, it was the first time in more than a hundred years that a Spanish prime minister had to share power with a coalition partner. That partner was Unidas Podemos, one of the parties founded in protest against the bitter medicine.

Indignados Everywhere

Just like in Spain, the financial crisis had thrown millions of people around the world into unemployment. And just like in Spain, spending cuts had crippled their safety nets. To breathe life into the economies, and to balance their austerity measures, governments jumped into action and printed trillions of dollars in new money to provide cheap credit to businesses. It seemed to work. Economies began to recover, just as promised. But hidden in the overall economic growth was the same growing inequality that had plagued Spain. Wages for workers stayed low even when corporate profits and stock prices soared. Trust in experts and institutions eroded as working- and middle-class people felt betrayed by what seemed more and more like a bailout for the rich. Within five months the Occupy Movement, an anticapitalist protest movement with tactics directly inspired by the *indignados'* occupation of squares in Barcelona and Madrid, spread to almost a thousand cities in eighty-two countries.[1]

A dangerous sentiment began to take hold that governments could not be trusted to put the needs of common people before those of banks and creditors. Frustration and distrust provided fertile ground for populism, conspiracy theories, and identity politics that promised ever more radical fixes with wide-ranging consequences. In Spain, antiausterity parties shook up a comfortable two-party political establishment. In the UK, it was the Brexit referendum in June 2016 that shook up the nation. This was followed by the election of Donald Trump in November the same year. These events marked not just a notable turn toward protest and populism, but in many countries also a turn away from truth.

The Icelandic Alternative

I am not an economist. But I believe that much pain could have been avoided if, instead of rushing to action, public leaders had slowed down to listen to those who would be affected by their vast rescue plans. Iceland showed us what such an alternative path might have looked like. Leaders in Iceland chose to put their citizens before the banks during the financial crisis. Instead of submitting to the demands of experts and lenders to bail out its banks and return to "normal," Iceland did what was deemed unthinkable in Spain: it let banks fail. Instead of austerity, Iceland implemented higher taxes for top earners while expanding its social safety net, reducing inequality.[2] And instead of rushing to action in 2010, the president of Iceland called for a referendum on whether to guarantee bank debts abroad.[3] Citizens were also invited to participate in drafting a new constitution. Admittedly, such listening is easier in a small country of just 330,000 citizens.

But the path paid off: Iceland's recovery was much faster

than expected. Youth unemployment in Iceland peaked at 15 percent in 2010 and dropped to 6 percent by 2016. Spain's youth unemployment peaked four years later, in 2014, at 55.5 percent and remained at a painful 33 percent in 2021. Slowing down to listen helped Iceland not only lower the pain for citizens, but it also delivered a much faster recovery. I like to think of this as *the dividend of slowness.*

A Flawed Fixation on Quick Fixes

As I reflect on the period following the 2007–2008 financial crisis, I see a simple pattern emerge. Whenever people in power—whether in business, activism, politics, or at home—try to rush to answers, they create divisions and produce failure. Our quest to improve things faster traps us like a hamster wheel. For more than twenty years, my job had been to feed that hamster wheel—to travel the world and tell people how to fix things faster. It was only when I opened up to slowness that I discovered a different way. All around me, I began to notice movements that were much better at solving our truly urgent problems. These slow-movers kept winning at the long game of pursuing audacious ideas by listening, extending trust, and patiently empowering others. The more I learned about them, the more I loved their way.

I call it the Slow Lane.

The Slow Lane and the Audacity of Empowerment

It is easy to overlook the Slow Lane in a world that celebrates only quick fixes. But the quick fixes offered by our leaders in business, government, or even at home often end up doing a lot more harm than good. In the Slow Lane, I found people who create solutions that don't simply patch over a problem but take aim at the injustices and broken systems that keep producing failure in the first place. Theirs is a sophisticated practice, at once bold in its vision and deeply committed to taking the time to engage in messy human needs. The result is progress that is truly transformational and inclusive.

The Fast Lane, Tailored for Dominance

Let me briefly remind you of how the Fast Lane works: a lot of things happen really fast around us. Amazon delivers in a day. Many apps give us instant gratification. New solutions come seemingly out of nowhere, and within a few years they are everywhere! The secret behind this speed is simple: focus on quick fixes and avoid anything that slows you down. This is the way of the Fast Lane. It is why people who can't get a credit card can't get an Uber. Tesla cars sell fast because they are for the rich. Facebook looks past hate speech or fake news on its own platform to grow faster.

But the things that would slow us down are often the hard truths about injustices, inequalities, or inequities in our society. By excelling at finding short-cuts around these issues, the Fast Lane only reinforces the divisions that plague us. A similar dynamic plays out in politics, when leaders assert their "leadership" by rushing to quick fixes that end up hurting millions, instead of engaging with the people whose lives are at stake. A perpetual cycle of solving one problem by creating another. Dominance means holding a powerful, controlling, or prevailing position over others. The Fast Lane is a product of a society that celebrates dominance as success. That's why, when we think about progress, we think of it mostly by the standards of the Fast Lane. Steve Jobs invented the iPhone, Jeff Bezos built Amazon, Elon Musk built disruptive electric car and space ventures. Why are these people the first to come to our mind? Why do we believe that this is what change looks like: heroic stories of disruption and dominance? As they impose their ideas on us, these visionaries inevitably break with the values we hold dear in our human relationships. And if success equals dominance, won't they choose speed and automation over inclusion and real conversation every time, feeding the divisions among us? The Fast Lane simply isn't designed to be an instrument of real change.

The Slow Lane: Change at the Speed of Trust

Things started to fall into place for me when I saw the work of User Voice at Pentonville Prison, a notorious prison in London. User Voice is a nonprofit that organizes ways for prisoners and ex-offenders to help improve the prison and probation services they receive. Theirs isn't a Fast Lane fix. User Voice brings ex-offenders into prisons, to find out what prisoners really need. They can do this because they're trusted. I realized that User Voice was moving in the opposite direction of the Fast Lane, slowing things down enough to carefully organize the kind of trusted conversation that brings people together until their needs are met. It is a template for how we can approach the many needs and problems overlooked by the Fast Lane. This kind of slowness is a sign of care, of true inclusion, of not being afraid to get involved with humans. It is also the kind of human mess that engineers and venture capitalists hate. But it works.

The Slow Lane is big. It is made up of millions of communities and movements, and the best way to understand it, is to observe how they work. I will mostly refer to them as "movements" in this book, but technically, they can take many shapes and forms: nonprofits, social enterprises, associations, networks, projects, alliances, groups, partnerships, nongovernmental organizations (NGOs), and foundations. The nonprofit User Voice, for example, initiated a movement that brings together prisoners, ex-offenders, their families, donors, health services, prisons, and their governors to better achieve the goal of the prison and probation system: successful rehabilitation. Like

User Voice, each movement in the Slow Lane has its specific purpose—a vision for change in which a social problem or need can be solved.

Slow Lane visions can appear outlandishly bold. For example, in 1970 it was unthinkable for a same-sex couple to be granted a marriage license in Minnesota. Homosexuality, at the time, was still classified by the American Psychiatric Association in its *Diagnostic and Statistical Manual of Mental Disorders* as a mental disorder.[4] And yet a Slow Lane movement had formed right there around the idea of marriage equality, leading to a predictably unsuccessful attempt in the same year by Jack Baker and Michael McConnell to obtain a marriage license.[5] Being the first, they had to fight their way to the Supreme Court—and lost. But they got the ball rolling, and forty-five years later, in 2015, the US Supreme Court ruled that all states must issue same-sex marriage licenses.

Countless movements in the Slow Lane today pursue such seemingly audacious goals. This book features some of the most instructional stories. Taken together, they offer us a glimpse of exciting new futures. But this boldness and persistence isn't a gimmick. It is an urgent reminder of the work still ahead of us. Slow Lane communities exist because the status quo remains intolerable for so many.

The Long History of Going Slow

For thousands of years, people have known the perils of rushing to action. Philosophers, religions, and folktales caution us against rushing to action. Many warn us of the arrogance that comes with moving fast. Aesop, the ancient Greek storyteller, created the fable of "The Tortoise and the Hare" that has inspired countless variations over time of a slow-mover (the tortoise) beating an arrogant sprinter (the hare). In Aesop's telling, the overconfident hare takes a long nap during the race,

letting the slow-and-steady tortoise arrive faster. The meaning
here is ambiguous. Is it a warning against arrogance, or a cele-
bration that perseverance and steadiness will prevail? In some
variants of the story, it is trickery that prevails, as is the case
in the Grimm's fairy tale "The Hare and the Hedgehog," where
the hedgehog places his similar-looking wife near the finishing
line. The incredulous hare demands revenge-runs over and
over, until he dies of exhaustion.

I, myself, am a relative latecomer to slowness, not paying
all too much heed to these tales. But as I began to see the Slow
Lane, it was Denisa Livingston, a friend and community health
activist in the Navajo Nation, who pointed me to the Slow
Food movement. I had come across Slow Food when I was a
teenager, passing a restaurant with a sign reading "No Fast
Food here, just Slow Food!" In my mind I had filed it away as
a snobby culinary alternative to fast food. But Denisa kindled
my curiosity, and I read up on the Slow Food movement. It had
grown into a global community of hundreds of thousands of
members promoting not just good food and wine but clean food
(meaning healthy to humans and the environment). And fair
food, referring to the treatment of the people involved in the
production and processing of food. Slow Food, I soon learned,
is a Slow Lane movement in and of itself. Over thirty-five years
the movement has evolved from a regional producers lobby in
Italy into a global human, economic, and environmental rights
movement. The kind of movement that now is a useful platform
even to Indigenous rights activists like Denisa. Slow Food is
only the most recognizable among many movements that promote slowness in fields like medicine, cinema, cities (cittaslow
network), fashion, technology, and travel.[6]

Daniel Kahneman's best-selling 2011 book, *Thinking, Fast
and Slow,* provided another compelling perspective.[7] It allowed
me to trace the Fast and Slow Lanes back to the dichotomy

between two systems of thought built right into our brains: one system is fast, instinctive, and emotional; the other is slower, more deliberative, and more logical. Kahneman, a professor of psychology, explains many irrational actions in society, business, the economy, and the military by how little effort it takes us to act fast. Thinking slow, he demonstrates, takes a lot more effort and energy. And people tend to avoid it, whenever they can. This insight is so foundational, that it changed the field of economics forever. He proved that by thinking fast, people will not behave rationally in their own best interest. Just like the quick-fixers of the Fast Lane keep producing undesirable outcomes. This work won him the Nobel Prize in 2002.

The Five Ways of the Slow Lane

After studying more than a hundred Slow Lane movements over the past two decades, I found that what really unifies the Slow Lane is not what these movements *do* but *how* they go about changing things. To avoid the kind of negative effects of the Fast Lane, these slow-laners adhere to a set of principles that guide their actions. My research led me to five Slow Lane Principles that stood out as universal and timeless. You will recognize them throughout the examples in this book. These principles are simple but can be practiced in sophisticated ways by people, movements, businesses, organizations, and even governments.

Slow Lane Principle #1: Hold the urgency

Don't sacrifice inclusion, participation, or sustainability for the sake of rushing to action. The Slow Lane strives to find solutions for everyone, in keeping with the ancient slogan "Nothing about us, without us," brought to life by disability activists around the world in the 1990s. Iceland did just that, when during the 2007–2008 financial crisis it resisted the impulse to restore the old order, and instead invited citizens to rewrite their constitution. Holding the urgency is to know that rushing to action won't get us there faster.

Slow Lane Principle #2: Listen

Don't pretend. Act with the humility to know the limitations of your listening. *How* you listen reveals whether you intend to treat others as equal contributors. User Voice broke the toxic power dynamics in the probation system by recruiting ex-offenders to do the listening. This kind of listening is essential to build the kind of trust that can change hearts and minds, allow something new to emerge, and keep people involved for the long haul.

Slow Lane Principle #3: Share the agency

Don't impose your answers. Create an environment in which even the least prepared people can find comfort and have the capacity, capability, and power to choose freely if they wish to join, contribute, and exert their power. User Voice engages and trains prisoners to give them a say in their rehabilitation journey. In the Slow Lane, empowerment is practiced with patience and care, meaning that this invitation meets people where they are and remains open to anyone at all times.

Slow Lane Principle #4: Nurture curiosity

Don't lock into a single answer. Curiosity makes the Slow Lane more inclusive and allows transformative visions to emerge. Curiosity lets us unlearn our preconceptions and open up to new ideas. Curiosity also lets us seek inspiration from outside our immediate reality—for example, from science or other movements. Without curiosity, User Voice might have become an activist prison rights movement that works against prisons, feeding on frustrated prisoners and their families. Instead, their lived experience and research revealed opportunities to work *with* prison leaders to improve outcomes for all. Curiosity helps movements retain the flexibility to find common ground.

Slow Lane Principle #5: Use technology as an enabler

Don't use technology to dominate others. Instead, develop strong human values, principles, and behaviors *that technology can enable*. Successful Slow Lane movements have rewritten the tech playbook to withstand the growth mind-sets that reduce complex human needs to what engineers believe they can solve. Tech in the Slow Lane is owned by everyone, and it uses creative new ways to enable the best in human relationships.

The following chapters explore how movements with very different missions have tailored the Slow Lane Principles to their needs, like parenting, data and technology, public service delivery, community development, health care, or waste management. The Slow Lane Principles are used so widely because they give communities the freedom to pursue whatever mission they have. They allow for diversity of thought and mission. They also create the kind of human dynamics we naturally enjoy and let us change things without doing harm to others. The Slow Lane Principles make us more resilient in the face of countless challenges and tempting opportunities. As we dive into the stories in this book, we will discover the beautiful and sophisticated ways in which these principles have been applied. This is all the more remarkable because the Slow Lane has no prescribed ideology, manifesto, law, or regulation. It has evolved as a practice because it works and comes naturally to so many.

Fast Failed. It's Time for the Slow Lane

As we emerge from a period of particularly challenging shocks to our lives, economies, democracies, and ecology, the Slow

Lane has only grown in importance. There was no war or natural catastrophe to blame as the cause of the financial crisis in 2007–2008. It was entirely man-made and laid bare a social and economic order that, to many people, felt unjust as they suffered through government austerity programs, public service cuts, and economic hardship. After decades of believing in a Fast Lane world of inventions, markets, and growth, many people have begun to see its limits. It offers no fix to what is broken in our communities. It seems only fitting that this period was capped by a global pandemic, unrest over persistent racism, and economic collapse hitting the most vulnerable people hardest.

More and more people are searching for alternatives. They want to move past this endless cycle of division and inequality. The Slow Lane offers a compelling alternative. It optimizes for what we know to be true social progress: care, respect, inclusion, justice, curiosity, humanity. It is a space of creativity, activism, and entrepreneurship that serves as our repository of social imagination. The Slow Lane Principles that connect its millions of disparate moving parts aren't new but the product of age-old wisdom. Its unifying idea is simple: meaningful social change is possible, and we can solve one problem without creating another. It is not surprising, then, that the Slow Lane is a system of staggering proportions. Millions of people, organizations, businesses, and governments are active in the Slow Lane today.

We can apply the Slow Lane Principles in the privacy of our family meal, at work, in our business, or when we step up in public. Personally, seeing these principles in action freed me to open up, listen, and trust that others will do right. It wasn't easy at first. I was brought up with strictly Fast Lane values, and like many entrepreneurs, developed a habit of inducing crisis to create urgency around my ideas. What else could be more important?

Trying on slowness felt like playing the trust fall, where you let yourself fall, hoping that someone will catch you. In this case I was hoping the Slow Lane would deliver. And there it was. Over and over, I found that when I stopped insisting on getting things done right away (= my way), new, much more creative outcomes became possible, as those around me really got a chance to contribute and express themselves. We built a community that got stronger every day. It was impossible to predict how long it would take or where it would lead. And some things never got done because they didn't matter at all.

I quickly learned a new habit: if it is really urgent, going slower will get me to the right place, faster.

How to Use This Book

The Slow Lane is a collection of stories and related insights, structured into seven chapters. Each story is written to offer an engaging insight into how change comes about. I have tried to avoid simply glorifying the successes in these stories but also to explore their inevitable setbacks and reveal the different ways by which the five Slow Lane Principles are put into practice.

The first five chapters each introduce a Slow Lane Principle, explaining how the principle is different from the way the Fast Lane works, then dive into stories that illustrate how the principle has been applied in successful movements. They are Chapter 1, "Hold the Urgency"; Chapter 2, "Listen"; Chapter 3, "Share the Agency"; Chapter 4, "Nurture Curiosity"; and Chapter 5, "Use Technology as an Enabler." Chapter 6, "Heal Democracy," explores how we can apply the Slow Lane Principles to strengthen our democracies, by avoiding divisive tactics and bringing more people to participate in ideas and decisions. Chapter 7, "Your Slow Lane," connects the dots across principles and scales to provide answers to the questions that help you put the Slow Lane to use. As a parent, as a leader, as a volunteer, in your movement, in business, and in government. The book's conclusion, "Where and How to Start," applies the first two Slow Lane Principles at different scales. Applying these two principles will unlock the path ahead through the other principles quite naturally.

= 1 =

Hold the Urgency

So, having solved this one set of things, but without
making fundamental shifts in how we ran the world,
we were setting ourselves up for much deeper trouble.

Bill McKibben

Rushing to action is the Fast Lane way to lead at a time of
crisis. That's how Spain's leaders acted following the financial crisis of 2007–2008. In this logic a good leader is strong
and decisive, one who shepherds their people through adversity and complexity. Quick fixes look compelling to Fast Lane
leaders, even if they sideline the nuance that consultation and
participation would bring. In business such leaders follow a
similar pattern as they rush to market dominance. That's how
Facebook, in its pursuit of growth, simply rushed past issues
like the proliferation of fake news or hate speech on its platform.

Since rushing to action is likely to cause harm, successful
Slow Lane movements opt for the opposite strategy. They hold
the urgency because they take a longer view. It is not that they
don't want change fast, or that they aren't in need of urgent
progress. But as a principle, Slow Lane movements strive not to
sacrifice inclusion, participation, and sustainability for speed.

Iceland picked this strategy during the financial crisis. Instead of restoring the old, broken order, leaders convened citizens to come up with the new order for the future. "Holding the urgency" is to know that the Slow Lane is the fastest way to get to the right place.

Three stories in this chapter explore how we can hold the urgency. The first story, "The Slow Race against Time," follows the story of the German environmental movement. Urgency was their main organizing principle: activists rushed into action to prevent the construction of Germany's nuclear power infrastructure. What was unusual was the movement's diverse make-up: conservative landscape conservationists and farmers fought alongside rebellious left-wingers and local families. Holding the urgency became essential to the success of the movement and the Green Party that emerged from it. And the Green Party went on to transform Germany's political system.

In "Division: Withstanding the Evil Temptation," the second story, we follow how Ireland ended up undoing 157 years of draconian laws that criminalized abortion. Peacefully. Why did public leaders not turn it into the kind of divisive issue that delivered quick wins for Republican leaders in the United States? What (and who) motivated them to hold the urgency, and lead the country to resolve this issue through patient deliberation? The third story, "Taming the Crisis in Our Homes," takes us to a dinner among my family and friends that turns sour when adults lose their cool over Fridays for Future. If Ireland can withstand the temptation of rushing to action, why is it so hard to hold our urgency at home? A conversation with my close friend Georg reveals the pressures we are under, when the fear for the future of our children clashes with our desire to provide answers, where none can be found. Put on the spot, the stakes seem unbearably high. Under pressure, we crack when it matters most.

Our fear of change in the face of crisis triggers reactions that stop many families, businesses, governments, and others from slowing down to care for and listen to one another. Put on the spot, our brains are wired to rush into action and to restore order, even when we know it is wrong. The way out? At times of great uncertainty, holding the urgency lets us accomplish important tasks together. Like finding alternatives and figuring out what those who matter most really need.

The Slow Race against Time

My first real memories start in the mid-1970s. At the time the evening news programs in West Germany were giving me the first glimpse of one of the nation's defining Slow Lane experiences. The daily *heute* evening news showed thousands of people desperately protesting against the construction of nuclear power stations. Men, women, local leaders, families, farmers, students. What were they doing? Up to one hundred thousand people, out in the rain, in muddy fields. Marching, blocking roads, chaining themselves to trees and railway tracks.

In those days most experts—scientists, engineers, and politicians—were proponents of nuclear power. Not only would it be the only way to guarantee economic growth, but nuclear power would be completely clean and safe. And yet, so many people were afraid. Afraid that accidents might happen, that radiation might leak into their fields or that families would get poisoned. Afraid of what to do with the toxic waste. What I didn't realize until much later is that one of the epicenters for these protests, the village of Brokdorf with fewer than a thousand inhabitants, was just outside my own home city of Hamburg. To me, on TV, what happened seemed worlds away.[1]

My personal relationship to this movement is no story of heroic activism. Quite the opposite. I grew up in a conservative-leaning home that had no time for these activists, who, I was told, were trying to undermine our national progress and energy independence. I came of age alongside the green movement in Germany. When I was four years old, in 1977, the green movement won its first parliamentary seat in a local election. The antinuclear movement founded the Green Party when it realized that it could not achieve real change through protest alone. By the time I was a young teenager, at school I noticed that some of my teachers were environmental activists. But instead of feeling inspired by their activism, I struggled to see past their political leanings and unfashionable looks. All this was too abstract for me.

What blinded me was that I had, unknowingly, already taken sides. I had lost sight of the problem they were trying to solve. In large part I think this was because my family had taken sides. At home we were not discussing environmental activism as a matter of ecology, climate change, nuclear power or its risks. It was talked about in terms of who was protesting, what lifestyle the protesters represented, their politics. At home we reduced the broad coalition, which included even conservative farmers, to the polarized politics of the industrial age two-party political system. You either were with business-friendly conservatives on the right or the Social Democrats backed by workers on the left.

With the protests looking a lot like left-wing student and social protests of the 1960s, and the fact that some of the movement's leaders had their roots in left-wing activism, our family, like many others, created a shorthand: environmentalism was just another complaint from the left. At our family meals the real measure of success was very much the Fast Lane world of business and dominance. Through that lens environmentalism was the realm of complainers who weren't succeeding in the economy, who had delusional ideas that would cripple business. These were people who would eat into the privileges of families like ours, who had worked hard and done well, who deserved the freedom to travel and consume as they liked.

Missing the First Signs

The year 1986 could have changed all that. In April, just months before my thirteenth birthday, we were glued to our TV screens as the nuclear catastrophe in Chernobyl unfolded just 1,600 kilometers away from our home. The dangers of nuclear power became real, as we experienced days of lockdown. Wind and rain had carried radioactive matter onto our streets and schoolyards (in fact, even today our family doctor in Berlin advised us not to eat local mushrooms, still contaminated from the fallout). That same year, in November, another environmental disaster unfolded on our TV screens. Efforts to extinguish a fire at the Sandoz chemical plant had washed toxic waste into the Rhine River, turning one of Europe's most scenic rivers an apocalyptic red and killing whole populations of wildlife.[2]

Many more Germans began to come around to the Green Party. In the national elections of 1987, it doubled its share of the vote. The movement had grown exponentially, it seemed, with protests now attended by hundreds of thousands of people. But even the meltdown at Chernobyl and the gruesome images of Sandoz didn't change my mind. I still couldn't see that these protesters, who had been going strong for more than a decade, were really onto something. Yes, these events did reveal the immense risk of nuclear and chemical technology, but it wasn't enough to shake off my prejudice against the movement. Fed by our family lore, and living in a city with no noticeable environmental risks, I continued to see the protesters as underachievers, do-gooders, and the butt of schoolyard jokes. My own social conscience was evolving in a different direction. I tried to come to terms with the social inequities around me, as well as the legacy of Germany's Nazi crimes.

And yet the environmental movement steadily kept making inroads into my life. As I studied architecture in the 1990s, a small but growing movement of architects and engineers took on the challenge of sustainable buildings and planning. For a long time, they too were belittled by the establishment, as reducing buildings to energy concepts. Here too, I went along and shared that view, seeing these architects and engineers as overly focused on finding engineering fixes for energy, instead of addressing the immense social, economic, and cultural inequities that I was passionate about. Living and working abroad, though, helped me overcome my prejudices against the people involved. Disconnected from my home politics and social dynamics, I began to lower my defenses to see environmentalism less as a type of people and more as a cause. The German Green Party, meanwhile, continued on a steady trajectory. By the time I was twenty-five, in 1998, they had become a major political force, joining the Social Democrats to form a new coalition government for Germany.

It Is All Connected, Stupid!

In 1995, I had my first chance to witness how intertwined inequality, suppression, economics, and environmental crimes often are. We were in South Africa less than a year after Nelson Mandela had become president, putting an end to the apartheid regime of racist white rule. For us, the visit was a field trip to work in the township of Riverlea in Soweto, on the outskirts of Johannesburg. Soweto had been created under the racist policies of South Africa in the 1930s and became the largest Black city in the country. But a South African township was nothing like a city.

For decades, millions of Black Africans had been forcefully resettled into townships like Soweto, where the population could only ever be temporary residents, serving as a workforce for Johannesburg. Racist ideology produced Soweto's urban plan, a layout more akin to a prison camp than a city. "Passion killer" floodlights illuminated Soweto like an airfield all night. Homes were built to the "Non-European 1951" (or NE 51/9) standard, with deliberately cynical, low-quality detailing.[3] In Riverlea, radioactive and poisonous waste from abandoned mines was piled into high mountains right around these poorly built homes, causing terrible respiratory diseases for generations.[4] When, in 1996, I went to work in the shanty towns of Caracas, I found the same dehumanizing confluence of severe social injustice and pollution.

In Germany, meanwhile, it took another major nuclear disaster—this time in Fukushima, Japan—for the government to finally mandate an end to nuclear power. It was almost impossible to argue for safety if a country like Japan, of no lesser engineering prowess than Germany, had so evidently lost control. Forty years of protests by a movement that had become the largest in German history, had thoroughly changed the social and political environment. Within days the cabinet announced a phasing-out of nuclear energy by the end of 2022.[5] At this point in 2011, the Green Party had become a third mainstream political force in Germany, polling at 25 percent in some states.

I had also changed, had come around to what these protesters had known all along: that the idea, that we could engineer ourselves out of our fossil fuel dependency through nuclear power, was just too risky (and too costly) in the face of unpredictable risks of global warming. And, more important, that this wasn't so much about the specific risks of a technology but the symptom of something broken in our society: our endless hunger for more growth and dominance. In 2021, as I returned to live in Germany after thirty years abroad, things went full circle as I cast my vote for the Green Party.

Wait, Not Everyone Can Be an Early Adopter

I had done next to nothing to help bring about this new ecological era. Instead, Brokdorf taught me a lesson in humility. For decades, I had missed the opportunity to look and think for myself, to be convinced by science and proven ideas. I beat myself up about it, afraid of what this revealed about me. But at other times I cut myself some slack. Had I not passionately pursued a different Slow Lane agenda that was just as meaningful?

We cannot possibly be early adopters and activists in every movement. And with time, just as I discovered how inseparable the social injustices I cared about were from environmental problems, the green movement became more embracing of social issues, especially once the fight against nuclear power in Germany was won. If, according to the environmentalist Barry Commoner, the first law of ecology is that "everything is connected to everything else," there is a good chance that different Slow Lane movements will converge over time, just as I had experienced.[6]

This is the truly important lesson to be learned: in some ways the green movement had been patiently waiting for me all along. Although they were always fighting against immediate and irreversible destruction, the movement held the urgency. Its focus on science and evidence meant that the movement expanded its following, building bridges into my life and work, instead of attacking me. Intentionally or not, the movement gave itself time to evolve and gave me the time it took to unlearn my prejudices, ideologies, and ideas of success in life.

A Very Unlikely Alliance

One thing that made the green movement in Germany special was that it was such an odd alliance. From the outset the movement broke with political left-right norms. On the left it was fueled by activists who had failed to realize their revolutionary dreams in the 1960s. They brought with them protest experience and tactics as well as participatory models that helped the antinuclear movement organize itself. But to the conservative political establishment, this history also linked them with leftist circles, at a time when Germany was experiencing a wave of radical leftist terrorism from the Red Army Faction (RAF) that culminated in the so-called German Autumn in 1977.[7] This fed a convenient narrative to cast the entire movement off as leftist radicals, when in reality the green movement had a much more diverse and mainstream membership: it included thousands of ordinary, politically moderate families and even very conservative groups such as farmers and landscape conservationists.

We cannot understand the impact, and unique trajectory, of the green movement in Germany without appreciating this unusual coalition of radicals, conservatives, concerned scientists, feminists, and families at a time of polarized politics. Geography was the force that united these groups. Germany is seven times more densely populated than the United States, meaning that any planned nuclear power station was going to be dangerously close to a population center. With so many people feeling at risk, the alliance became a very practical arrangement around specific locations. Protests were organized at these planned nuclear sites, places like Brokdorf, which in turn provided a physical space and opportunity for these groups to have shared experiences in mass protest and activism. For many people these experiences included aggressive policing by a state that was desperate to uphold its dominance.

A Pressure Cooker of Inclusiveness

Outside their shared mission, there was plenty of distrust among these different groups. Who should lead? What happened behind closed doors? This was a grassroots movement caught up, on live television, in a pressure cooker of history: the Cold War induced fear of socialism and nuclear threats, internal conflicts raged among the radical urban left and conservative members, and real-time events like Chernobyl and Sandoz drew attention to the cause. These circumstances forced the movement to constantly reinvent its tactics and develop new ways to make decisions. Weary of self-proclaimed leaders, the movement established rules to reassure and empower every activist. Unlike the more homogenous movements of the 1960s, this inclusive approach tempered the more radical activist instincts to cast the world into irreconcilable "us" and "them" logics. It is a defining characteristic that would be carried over for decades and eventually kept the doors open to latecomers like myself.

I am making a simple point here. This early pragmatism around a common cause led to a culture of listening, debate, inclusiveness, and resistance to traditional forms of hierarchy that had defined the political establishment of the 1970s. In my view, much of the long-term resilience and later political success of the Green Party goes back to this strange initial coalition that was so full of distrust. The Green Party is known for its extensive debates between realists (Realos) and fundamentalists (Fundis), which averaged out to a tense form of moderation. It revolutionized political practices in Germany, by institutionalizing procedures that require direct participation in major decisions by all party members, by creating rules to resist the aggregation of power by professional politicians, and by instituting a 50 percent quota for women in party leadership roles and elections.

A Slow Race against Time

Germany's green movement never was complacent or intentionally slow. Quite the opposite. Urgency has been central to the movement from its inception: to stop nuclear construction projects, harmful policies, or emissions before it was too late. But its diverse founding history forced the movement to mediate between urgency and inclusiveness. Even today, the Green Party regularly struggles through difficult debates over principles, urgency, and pragmatism. But despite the imperfection of politics, it has institutionalized inclusive practices that resonate with the Slow Lane. What started out as a resistance movement of outliers has evolved into an established political force. The Green Party's unique way of involving grassroots members in decisions means that many more ordinary people are involved in weighing the pursuit of politically riskier quick wins against the long-term success of its socioecological agenda.

Germany's green movement is no simple success story. In 2019 Germany's overall CO emissions per person were the fifth-highest among European Union countries; Germany was ranked twenty-fifth among the world's highest emitting people.[8] German politicians were direct and indirect enablers of what became known as "Dieselgate," the Volkswagen diesel emissions scandal, a systematic fraud perpetrated by the all-powerful auto industry that undermined the nation's green credentials. This Slow Lane journey is still a work in progress, and who knows how long it will take. But it is indisputable that the green movement has already made a truly important contribution to democracy, releasing Germany from a two-party system that was defined not by the future but by ideologies anchored in its industrial past.

Division: Withstanding the Evil Temptation

For centuries, public leaders have resorted to a distasteful instrument to get their way, fast. Division. They follow a simple yet effective playbook: look for something only "their people" have in common, then single out the "others," who are now declared inferior. Whip up an urgent sense of a sacred, existential mission that justifies any means. History is full of terrible events that used this playbook: wars, civil wars, sectarian violence, genocide, identity politics, the Holocaust. For examples, we don't need to look far back into history. Think Brexit, think Rwanda, think Trump, think Scottish or Catalan independence, think the fight over abortion rights in America. Division does nothing to heal or enrich democracy. In all these cases public leaders chose division as an effective way to preserve their power or get their next big win. For communities it is a downward spiral that is hard to escape.

Why, then, did public leaders in Ireland pick a different path to tackle their country's most divisive issue? A socially conservative catholic country, Ireland took the Slow Lane to remove a draconian ban on abortion from its constitution.

The Eternal Temptation

Before we get to Ireland and its peaceful settlement on abortion in 2018, I want to take you back to an experience I had in Barcelona in 2012. It is a reminder of the lure of identity politics. One morning, in my neighborhood square, a group of pro-independence political activists called me over to their information stall. They asked me if I was going to vote for Catalan independence from the Spanish state in the upcoming referendum. "Why," I asked, "would I?" I was with my daughters, eight and five years old, at the time. Both had been born and raised in Barcelona, had spoken Catalan as their first language at kindergarten and school for years. At home we sang Catalan nursery rhymes.

Upon hearing my question, the activists lost interest. After all, I had replied in Spanish, not Catalan. It may not sound like much, but this was the first time, after a decade of living in Barcelona, that I had the courage to ask a pro-independence activist to pitch me. I never dared ask until then because whenever conversations turned to Catalan nationalism, immigrants like myself were told to shut up in no uncertain terms. We were told that we would never understand because we weren't Catalan. But why weren't we?

When What Divides Us Trumps Everything

When we first moved to Barcelona in 2002, the region's nationalism had felt benign. It felt like a way of preserving a regional identity, celebrating the language and culture. As my children were born there, I began to wonder. Were we now Catalan, too? Or just the girls? Things really began to change when the financial crisis of 2007–2008 brought to light serious financial mismanagement and political corruption in the region.[9] As the scandal unfolded, the otherwise moderate regional president Artur Mas tried to divert attention by conjuring up Catalan nationalist sentiment.[10] According to Mas, it wasn't a matter of finance or corruption but of "us" (the Catalans) against "them" (the Spanish, who had called out the financial mismanagement).

What for years had felt like a welcoming regional identity began to turn more overtly divisive by the day. In a speech Mas even referred to the "Catalan DNA" as being non-Spanish.[11] The 2012 "informal" independence referendum divided society further. At school some children refused to speak Spanish. Families were divided. Politicians took more and more polarizing positions, forcing voters to choose parties on the single issue of identity. Public leaders seemed to answer my question for me: immigrants like us were at best an afterthought in the independence project. In matters of identity, bloodlines trumped all else.

Years later, in 2018, I learned about the constitutional referendum in Ireland that legalized abortion. Now living in America, we had lived through a bruising and divisive

presidential election that brought Donald Trump to the presidency. And in other countries there had been a series of ref-
erendums that were notable mostly for their false and divisive
claims, like those for Scottish and Catalan independence as
well as for Brexit. The results from Ireland caught my attention.
They were soothing because they seemed so orderly. Instead of
dividing society, the results seemed to offer a path for us to
tackle even sensitive issues. The story of Ireland holds some
valuable clues as to how people in power can withstand the
temptation of rushing to divisive action.

A 157-Year Journey to Empowerment

First, a quick history of what happened in Ireland. In 1861 the
Parliament of the United Kingdom of Great Britain and Ireland
passed the Offenses against the Person Act that penalized abortion with imprisonment with hard labor for life for the woman,
and three years for anyone found aiding an attempted abortion.
The legislation remained in place in predominantly Catholic
Ireland and was reinforced by the Eighth Amendment to the
Irish constitution in 1983 after pro-life campaigners feared a
judicial ruling against the draconian 1861 law. The Eighth was
supported by the three main political parties of the time and
approved by 66.9 percent of the population in a referendum. It
was only in 2018 that the legislation was removed, replaced by a
law permitting abortion, as the result of a national referendum
in which 66.4 percent of Irish voters voted in favor of legalizing
abortion. Ireland had settled a painfully divisive issue peacefully, strengthening democracy along the way.

The Right Activist, in the Right Place, at the Right Time

Many people who have studied this history told me about
Katherine Zappone, whom they considered a central figure in

the story. As I connected via Zoom with Katherine in her home in New York City, I had two questions on my mind. I wanted to know why Ireland had *not* made abortion a matter of eternal political division. And I wanted to know what had led to this peaceful resolution. Like so many key players in the Slow Lane, Katherine's life story matters.

Born in Seattle, Katherine became a theologian and moved to Ireland in 1982, just months before the introduction of the Eighth Amendment. She was a self-described feminist. Her partner (and later wife) was the theologian Ann Louise Gilligan, a former nun. Together, they founded An Cosán in 1986, one of Ireland's largest providers of education and services to empower women and girls from disadvantaged areas. Teaching feminist theology in Ireland, Katherine found that the Eighth took a central role in her work. The issue eventually forced her out of Catholic institutions. She joined Ireland's leading nonreligious university instead.

Katherine became a leading advocate for better abortion rights and marriage equality. Her first success came about in 1992, when a referendum stopped the introduction of even more hardline clauses to the constitution and led to amendments that allowed sharing information about abortion services abroad. It took twenty-one years until advocates could claim the next win, the 2013 Protection of Life During Pregnancy Act. In 2016, Katherine became an independent member of parliament and joined the cabinet of Prime Minister Enda Kenny as minister for Children and Youth Affairs. Katherine's appointment was essential to the prime minister, who needed her vote to form a minority government. Katherine, who didn't see eye to eye on most issues with this socially conservative politician, had a single condition to join his government: she demanded a citizen assembly on abortion reform.

The Path of Peaceful Deliberation

To learn about this citizen assembly, I called Jane Suiter, a professor of communications at Dublin City University and one of the leading scholars on citizen assemblies in Ireland. I wanted to know why, of all things, Katherine had demanded a citizen assembly. Jane told me that since the 1983 adoption of the Eighth, the harsh terms of the law had created a growing number of legal challenges. High-profile cases revealed the inhumane conditions the law created for victims of rape and for women and girls in other life-threatening situations. Even the United Nations Human Rights Committee called on Ireland to do something about a law that was exceptionally cruel to women.[12] But the dominant political parties, all socially conservative, had little appetite for an issue that the media portrayed only in its extremes.

Meanwhile, Jane and her colleagues in political science departments at different Irish universities had grown increasingly concerned about the decline in political debate. In 2009 they formed a working group to develop new ways forward. In 2011 they organized We the Citizens, the first experimental citizen assembly.[13] The goal was to find a way to slow down decision-making on critical and divisive issues and to avoid political posturing by letting randomly selected citizens develop recommendations. We the Citizens inspired an act of parliament in 2012 that established a first national citizen assembly, the Irish Constitutional Convention.[14] It was a new forum for deliberation, made up of one hundred people. One of the most notable outcomes was a recommendation that led to the legalization of same-sex marriage in a national referendum on May 22, 2015. Katherine hoped that such a citizen assembly could find a peaceful resolution for abortion, too.

Here is how the citizen assembly that led to the abolition

of the Eighth Amendment worked. In 2016 the Irish government created a citizen assembly, modeled on the experience of
the Constitutional Convention. The assembly was chaired by
Justice Mary Laffoy, a respected former supreme court judge.
Ninety-nine members would be invited to develop recommendations for the parliament on eight themes. As demanded by
Katherine, the Eighth Amendment was one of them. Thirty-
three of the assembly members were appointed by political parties in parliament. Sixty-six members were ordinary citizens
selected at random by a jury, to be representative of different
social, economic, and geographic backgrounds. Before deliberations commenced, an open call invited the public to present
their views. They presented thirteen thousand submissions.

Irish Citizen Assembly

Mary Laffoy, the chair, invited seventeen organizations to make
presentations to the assembly, representing different sides of
the abortion debate. Members met to hear presentations, con-
sulted experts, and deliberated for eighteen months before the
assembly voted on its recommendations for constitutional reform. The recommendations reflected the different views of the
assembly. Options included abolishing or reforming the Eighth
as well as views on the application of time limits for abortion
relative to the age of the fetus, and consideration of other circumstances such as rape or health risks to women. The government led a debate of the recommendations in parliament, as
mandated by law.

In May 2018 the government presented the abolition of the
Eighth for a constitutional referendum. And 66.4 percent of
voters came out in favor of abolishing the Eighth. A new law,
the Regulation of Termination of Pregnancy Act, was adopted
at the same time to legalize abortion for up to twelve weeks of
gestation.

The Phone Call That Put an End to Fast Leadership

According to Jane, the experience of poor decision-making during the financial crisis played a major role in making the citizen assemblies possible. In 2008, facing the collapse of the financial system, government leaders in Ireland had found themselves in a similar position to leaders in Spain. In an ad-hoc phone meeting at six in the morning, the cabinet decided to guarantee all banks. A decision that would cost Irish taxpayers billions and cause years of hardship was taken by phone, in a rush, with no meaningful evidence or consultation. In part, this rushed decision came about because leaders felt that the public expected decisive leadership. But later, after the fallout became clear, citizens were looking for a different way. Citizen assemblies offered one such new way forward, a way in which citizens could participate in big, complex, and nuanced decisions.

Building Back Better Belief Systems

Another important enabler of the citizen assembly was that following the financial crisis, Ireland found itself grappling with its values. Before the collapse, Ireland self-proclaimed its fast growth economic model as the Celtic Tiger. The nation's leaders had hoped that by unleashing financial markets and globalization, Ireland would deliver sustainable wealth and progress. But the financial crisis only brought humiliation, austerity, and grief. When I attended Ashoka's Change Nation summit in Dublin in 2012, I heard public leaders discuss their sense of shame over what had happened in the Celtic Tiger years. Shame in letting greed and speculation go so far, and a sense that their decision-making (including the 6 a.m. phone conference to bail out the banks) had served financial over human needs. It was an incredible moment of reckoning.

Here was a nation coming to terms with its Fast Lane ways that had led it astray from its tradition of humility and neighborly values. People wanted a better way forward.

The third enabler of Ireland's transformative citizen assemblies was the rapid decline of influence from the Catholic Church. Starting in the late 1980s, historians, journalists, activists, commissions, and parliamentary inquiries revealed a seemingly endless history of abuse of women and children by the church.[15] By challenging the purity of the rigid doctrines of the past, these revelations made room for rebalancing people's religious beliefs and human rights. Ireland was a late mover compared with other European countries on both investigating abuse and carrying out reforms. Katherine and activists like her found themselves not just demanding change but also cushioning this transition from a country organized around the church, to a country organized around human rights. As a feminist, the first openly gay cabinet minister, and a theologian married to a former nun, Katherine's life embodied this transition. As a theologian and trusted member of the prime minister's cabinet, she was able to shepherd government leaders through their difficult questions of faith.

Real Division Was Always Just a Short Drive Away

What happened in Ireland was no accident. It had been in the making, crawling toward resolution for generations. More than a matter of abortion laws, it was a symptom of broken societal systems holding back progress on human rights. As to my question of why politicians had not used abortion to divide (and rule) the country, as they had done in America, both Katherine and Jane couldn't provide any real answers.

Here is what I think. Northern Ireland must have played into it. Belfast is just a two-hour drive from Dublin. When I visited West Belfast shortly before the Good Friday Agreement that brought peace to Northern Ireland in 1998, I saw a glimpse of what can happen when you go all in on the game of division. High walls separated Catholic and Protestant communities after decades of sectarian violence. Police trucks with snipers patrolled Catholic neighborhoods in an attempt to control the Troubles, the uprising against British rule of Northern Ireland. Neighborhood police stations were fortified like bunkers in a war zone. Taxis were either serving Catholic or Protestant neighborhoods. Military cordons protected children on their way to school. It was a city divided. And a reminder for leaders in Dublin to not gamble everything but play it slow.

A Roller-Coaster, a Crash, an Elegant Landing

The deep soul-searching that Ireland underwent following the financial crises, coupled with the Catholic abuse crises, must have contributed to the peaceful and inclusive reform of abortion laws. It was a moment of reckoning but also of unlearning. Too many people had made mistakes, had misplaced trust, had believed in economic growth, had looked the other way. Like many other countries, Ireland got its wake-up call. Unlike others, Ireland chose to slow down by creating citizen assemblies to deliberate these complex questions. And these citizen assemblies got things done and proved productive. Over the course of a decade, Ireland passed a series of important constitutional and policy reforms.

Unlike Spain, it wasn't radical new political parties that uprooted the Irish political establishment. Mind-sets and belief systems had shifted from within, helped along by widely respected institutions, universities, and movements. People like Justice Mary Laffoy, Katherine Zappone, and Jane Suiter stepped up to fill the void. They offered guidance when long-held power structures and belief systems fell apart. The citizen assembly was the kind of instrument that helped steer the final phase of this pivotal period to a resolution, holding the urgency until the end.

Taming the Crisis in Our Homes

The stories of how Iceland and Ireland took to their citizens, and how the German environmental movement held the balance between urgency and inclusion, give us insights as to how leaders can hold the urgency to tame moments of crisis. After all, these countries withstood the temptation of quick, authoritarian fixes in the face of collapsing financial markets, international pressure, and fear of nuclear disaster. And they remind us of what is lost when people in power give in to these temptations: millions of people suffer.

Even as we know all this, holding the urgency can prove elusive when we are among our loved ones. It is worth exploring how things can play out in the safety of our homes because it reveals how taking part in the Slow Lane also calls for important inner work.

A Fraught Family Dinner Conversation

Spain, 2019. It was a beautiful summer evening. We had set a table underneath the olive tree, overlooking the sea. It was a special treat for us to be among old friends, since we had left Europe to live in New York four years earlier. Our daughters, seated among us at the table, were all young teenagers now. Everyone was lending a hand, the conversation was fun and easygoing, as it can only really be when you are in the company of people you trust. I noticed how Olivia, my then eleven-year-old daughter, was looking around the table waiting for an opening to say something. She was shy in front of adults, but at last she spoke up. "At school, my friends and I have started to learn about Fridays for Future," she said. "We have even joined some of the marches in New York. Our teachers and some parents who are scientists have helped us learn more about climate change. I think it is really urgent we do something."

It was true, since the beginning of the year, the girls' growing interest in climate change had had some real impact in our family. First, they went vegetarian, and I saw almost daily how they grappled with balancing their desire for things with their carbon footprint. "In just a few weeks," Olivia continued, "we will have a really big climate march in New York. I think Greta Thunberg, who started Fridays for Future, will be there also!" Now the other Olivia, my good friend Georg's twelve-year-old daughter, chimed in.[16] "Same here! My friends and I also participate in Fridays for Future at home in Barcelona." As the girls shared their excitement about Fridays for Future, the mood at the table changed. Visibly agitated, Georg jumped into the conversation. "I hate any form of personality cult, and this is exactly what this Greta has become. This hasn't played well in the past. Also, Greta is autistic, so there must be someone who is telling her what to say! She's just a puppet, and teens are just blindly falling for her." Soon, several of the grownups joined in and laid into Fridays for Future and Greta Thunberg. They looked defensive, their faces red. They no longer talked to the two Olivias but debated among themselves.

Then, quite abruptly, the evening ended in an awkward silence. The girls left to hang out. As we cleared the table, Georg, like the other grownups, looked uncomfortable.

What Stopped Us from Listening, When It Mattered Most?

A year had passed when I called Georg to ask if he would be comfortable revisiting the evening with me, to understand why things had happened the way they did. To me, that night revealed something about our relationship to change. "You know, I feel very strongly that Greta Thunberg is a distraction, that she is divisive, polarizing, and not building bridges," Georg said. "I have a real aversion to this kind of idolizing of leaders, to have people who symbolize a cause. I don't know, maybe it is to do with being German, because of our history." He explained that he prefers answers that are more nuanced, technocratic, and science-based. To Georg, it feels dangerous when young people are enthralled by a personality they only know from social media and who is promoting such uncompromising demands.

But as the conversation progressed, I noticed how Georg took longer pauses, becoming more pensive. "Maybe there was also something else that caused me to react the way I did," he said. "I can't quite put my finger on it. I think I felt a bit overwhelmed, put on the spot. Vulnerable. It was a terrible feeling. I may have felt that I don't have any real answers to the threat climate change poses to our children. But at the same time, as a father, I am supposed to protect them, know all the answers."

Georg and I had become close friends over the twelve years that I lived in Barcelona. He is incredibly thoughtful, and I admire his work as a successful photographer working for magazines, spending time with journalists and traveling all over the world. As a teenager, I had dreamed of becoming a photographer, like him. Both of us had grown up in quite similar circumstances, moderately conservative households, in what was West Germany at the time.

I asked Georg whether, if he had known beforehand that we would talk about Fridays for Future that evening, he would have handled the conversation differently. "Yes. No doubt," he said. "I don't think I would have got caught up on the credibility of Greta Thunberg. I mean, the evening was about the girls sharing their enthusiasm for a civic cause. It seems shortsighted, in hindsight, to try to discredit the movement or win an argument against the girls. It should have been a moment to celebrate that our daughters spoke up about a cause they cared about."

Georg told me that with a moment's time to reflect, he might have seen the bigger picture. "I should have helped them, first and foremost, by listening and engaging with their ideas. There would also have been no harm admitting that I myself was afraid also. That I don't know the answers. It would have been nice to open the door to an ongoing conversation with them about how we can change things. You know, they actually know a lot."

Georg's words resonated not just with my experience as a parent but also with my professional experiences. Fear of change in the face of crises triggers reactions that stop so many families, businesses, governments, and others from slowing down to listen to one another. Put on the spot, we rush to restore order, even when we know it is wrong. To restore order, we assert ourselves by tapping into stereotypes, prejudice, and posturing that has been cultivated for generations.

According to my friend Eric Dawson, founder of the youth-empowerment group Peace First, 99 percent of media coverage consumed (and produced) by adults presents young people as either a problem or a victim. This feeds a preconception among adults that young people have nothing to contribute. It is not surprising, then, that in Australia, for example, only 3.3 percent of news articles featured young people and that two-thirds of young Australians feel that mainstream media has no idea what their lives are like.[17]

Sadly, shutting out others and rushing to action is the norm in how we deal with our fear of losing control. Behavioral scientists such as the Nobel Prize–winning psychologist Daniel Kahneman have shown that people all too often behave in ways that are contrary to their best interest. It is in moments of crisis—whether in our economy, our business, or at a family dinner—that we rush to actions we subsequently come to regret because we stopped listening to those who matter most.

Slowness, Bad and Good

Isn't it interesting how time reveals itself as almost secondary in these stories of leaders, movements, and people holding their urgency? They all respond to crises; they all want to change things fast. And yet, their urgency operates more like fuel than a hard delivery date. Even in the German green movement (where urgency was the actual purpose!), urgency turned out to provide the energy that was channeled into creating something much bigger. It motivated people to keep experimenting with different forms of organizing, testing, and adapting different forms of action, and ultimately helped them reshape the entire political system.

For powerful leaders in business and politics, there is a choice to be made: they can either hold their urgency, or take the Fast Lane of quick fixes. Leaders in Spain, Iceland, and Ireland had that kind of power. My friend Georg appeared to have this power too, at our dinner table, when he chose to rush into action and judgment. But hindsight revealed how his reaction was fueled by a deeper sense of helplessness, of losing control. His frustration, his sense of powerlessness, was shared by the environmental activists in Germany and the women's rights campaigners in Ireland. They all wanted "change right now." But it was simply beyond their control to determine the speed or direction of change. They found themselves holding the urgency not as a matter of choice but as the only way to develop the kind of critical mass that could lead to change. For these activists slowness is a double-edged sword. It causes pain and anger, but it also unlocks far bigger success later on.

Slow Down to Get Important Things Done

As painful as it may be, holding the urgency lets us accomplish important things. It helps us figure out what "good" should really look like. Spain's bitter medicine wasn't just cruel, it was also unimaginative. It immediately reduced the crisis and its moment of uncertainty to a single task: return the financial system to what it was before, at any cost. Leaders lost all sense of proportion when they failed to ask, "At what cost?" They showed no desire to imagine an alternative, to imagine a better outcome than taking away the dignity of millions as they descended into poverty. Spain's *indignados*, camping on city squares, created movements that began to fill that lack of imagination with new answers. They tried to do in a couple of years what the German green movement did over the course of five decades: to dream up a different future. For them, slowing down created a new political platform to imagine better answers.

Holding the urgency also lets us build bridges. As movements strive to realize their visions, they need allies. Germany's green movement and Ireland's human rights activists became ever more inclusive. Building such bridges can be very uncomfortable, as many movements start out by creating an identity of being different, creating an us against them mentality. Successful movements avoid such division. Activists in Germany realized that they couldn't insist that people submit to a predefined set of ideas. That turned out to be wise because such indoctrination rarely works. Instead, these activists invented a new, more participatory way of running a political party. Eventually its unique way of making decisions created a powerful logic, by which even newcomers and outsiders are seen as fully capable contributors.

But here is the challenge: holding the urgency feels counterintuitive at a time of crisis. From a young age we grow up learning how powerful it is to conjure up a crisis to get things done. After all, a crisis permits us to grab power and resort to special, often authoritarian measures.

What Made Them Slow Down?

What made these leaders slow down? Hidden in these stories are different reasons why some leaders grasped the value of holding the urgency. In Iceland, a small country, bailing out the banks would have drowned its small population in debt. Being a small island nation outside the European Union and its single currency may have given Iceland that bit of additional room for common sense and independent thinking. Unlike leaders in Spain, leaders in Iceland realized that it was above even their pay grade to make a decision of such magnitude *for* people and not *with* people. Calling a constitutional assembly also echoed the kind of soul-searching that people in Ireland experienced when it reckoned with its Celtic Tiger years of fast growth, greed, and speculation. And this soul-searching wasn't all that different from Georg's reflections on why he ended up that evening long ago saying the polar opposite of what he really wanted to do.

We can be more intentional. We now know, after all, that holding the urgency will get us to the right place faster. With that knowledge we can say "Hold on!" when we are told that there is no alternative and that a high price must be paid. Let's just assume that there always is an alternative, but that to imagine it, we may have to let go of something we hold dear. Like our pride in having always been right, or admitting that going back is not an option. As we practice slowing down in this way, we should be compassionate with ourselves and those around us. Our brains, after all, are literally wired to rush to action, looking for old answers to new problems.

The Joy of Slowness

As we overcome the temptation of quick fixes, we can push our imaginations to new heights—whether at home in our families, in our communities, at work, in business, in government or society. This is fun, and it is energizing. One of the secrets to success in the Slow Lane is to create enough joy to see us through the inevitable setbacks until we reach the other side. That moment when our big dreams become the new norm.

To get there, however, we need to do more than slow down a bit, here and there. We need to say, "I am not going anywhere!" Staying for as long as it takes. Isn't that what caring is all about?

= 2 =

Listen

Radical change...doesn't start with yelling. It starts
with deliberation, a tempo that increases, a volume set
first at a whisper. How else can you begin to picture
what doesn't yet exist?

Gal Beckerman

I suspect that you are a bit like me, when it comes to listening: you know that it is vital to relationships and to improve things in an inclusive and respectful manner. In this chapter we dive into what it really takes to listen, and how easy it is to just pretend.

When it comes to listening, *pretending* is how it's done in the Fast Lane. There, powerful people or institutions create what we might call a theater of listening. They perform in a way that looks like they are listening on the surface, and they may even believe that they are listening, but they aren't listening in a way that leads to actual change. Like all quick fixes, the pretending has a lot going for it: in essence, you wait just long enough to hear what others have to say and then you get back to doing what works for you. But there is only so much pretending we can do without really meaning it. Behind the theater, how listening is done in the Fast Lane reveals a lot about its true intentions. It isn't just a matter of holding the urgency, of taking more time. An engineer at Facebook, for example, practices really intense listening by collecting tons of data about users to predict their needs and manipulate them into spending more time looking at ads, not to help users lead better lives.

Really meaning it, when it comes to listening, is a hard nut to crack. In this chapter about listening, we begin in the most unlikely of places. The first story, "Enlightenment on The Cally," follows the story of User Voice, a nonprofit run by ex-offenders. They have developed a new model of listening to break down toxic power dynamics in which prisoners participate in improving conditions in an overcrowded and violent prison. From Pentonville Prison we move to the intimacy of my home. At home, listening should be easiest. Yet in "What's Your Favorite Color? Blue or Blue?" I end up wondering whether I am the prison governor in my daughters' lives, as I unpack the power dynamics behind my Saturday Question. This story reveals an uncomfortable truth about how easy it is to cheat yourself into believing that you're listening. The final story in this chapter, "The Slow Lane Government," takes us to the city of Sefton in the UK. Here, decades of financial and economic hardship have led leaders to build a truly listening government, where citizens are not seen as people with problems but trusted contributors to improve services and make the city more resilient.

Each of these stories offers a piece of the puzzle of how to put real listening into practice. To truly listen at home, in our businesses, in our movements, in our governments requires us to be honest about our intentions toward those around us and let go of our fears. And some of our power.

Enlightenment on The Cally

London, 2014. I was strolling up the Caledonian Road, or The Cally as locals lovingly call it. As I left London's futuristic Kings

Cross Station behind, small boarding houses, betting shops, letting agents, fish-and-chips shops, off licenses, kebab shops, vegetable stores, and community pubs took turns along the streetscape. I crossed a canal lined by trees. Walking up The Cally was like traveling back to a time when Central London still had working-class neighborhoods. It had always been, awkwardly, both conveniently central and undesirable at the same time. People lived in apartments above the small shops, public housing from all kinds of periods, terraced homes. And then, an abrupt change. After about a mile, massive walls emerged, towering between the small homes. Three stories of solid brickwork, a barrier almost a mile long, topped by barbed wire. A dystopian Victorian fortress. Even if you lived right next to it, it would have been impossible to know what exactly happened behind these walls. I had arrived at my destination.

Pentonville Prison had been largely unchanged since 1842, when it was built to house five hundred prisoners awaiting deportation and held in isolation. The prison had always been notorious, feeding scandalous headlines. Most recently, it had made the news for murder, crumbling cells, overcrowded conditions for its thirteen hundred prisoners. There was even a scandal involving drones delivering drugs to inmates from the air. As I walked in, the entrance area felt weirdly like a small-town police station. Even as a visitor, I felt like I was leaving a piece of myself behind with every door and gate we passed. Everything I carried on me went into a small locker. My phone, keys, wallet, camera, passport. I couldn't help feeling powerless. *Do I need to watch what I say? What if they were to just keep me in here?*

Inside, a warden took me and the other members of our group of visitors through a common area surrounded by cells to our destination, an ordinary meeting room set with tables, coffee, and a few snacks. My excitement had grown for some time as I anticipated the event that was about to take place here. Kevin Reilly, known as the No. 1 Governor and the top official in charge of running the prison, would soon meet with prisoner representatives to hear their ideas for improvements to prison life. For the people of Pentonville Prison, this was a big deal. For weeks, prisoners had run an election to select their representatives, who in turn had prepared a list of ideas for improvement to present to the governor today. We were here to attend the prison council, the first such meeting in the 172-year history of Pentonville Prison.

Humility had brought Kevin Reilly to the table. Cuts to government budgets, the result of years of austerity after the 2007–2008 financial crisis, meant that for some time now he didn't have enough money to run the prison properly. People who in the past might have accepted a job working in the prison now found more attractive jobs in other, better funded areas of public safety. He had trouble filling his job openings. Short of funds and staff, he couldn't keep his facilities in good enough shape, or provide all that is needed to treat prisoners in a humane way. All this made the prison more dangerous. Rising tensions caused more problems for him, including scandalous headlines. It was a vicious circle that he hoped to break by chairing the prison council. Kevin Reilly had come to give prisoners a say in how the prison's scarce resources should be used.

None of us would be in this room if it hadn't been for User Voice, a nonprofit from London. User Voice organizes prison councils and has developed other trusted ways to let users of probation services—both in and out of prison—contribute to improvements. User Voice had come up with the idea, and Pentonville was only the latest in a growing list of prisons across the country that had set up prison councils. User Voice helps the prison system by collecting high-quality feedback from prisoners to improve conditions. Better conditions meant, among other benefits, that prisoners could focus on preparing for life after incarceration.

Before Mark Johnson started User Voice, he had lived many of the experiences shared by prisoners in Pentonville. In *Wasted*, a book about his childhood, youth, and early adulthood, Mark recalls his tragic and complicated story of surviving violent domestic abuse as a child and how he slipped into crime and addiction.[1] For years, he had lived homeless on the streets of central London, feeding a $600-a-day heroin addiction. Mark had been in and out of prison himself. After a long struggle he broke free from addiction and crime. He discovered his previously hidden potential when he started building award-winning businesses. But Mark found his true calling when in 2009 he started User Voice to help others have a fair chance as they struggle on their journey to rehabilitation.

Over coffee, I asked Joe from User Voice about what it took to make this prison council happen. "It took forever," he told me. "We have tried for years to set up a prison council here. But Kevin and the current prison management finally gave us the green light." Changing things in government is hard. It must be harder still in a prison. "We at User Voice are all ex-offenders," Joe explained. "I've done time myself. It takes open-minded people like Kevin to let us run a program like this." He nodded in the direction of the prisoner representatives. "It is a bit of an art to recruit the right people to stand for election. People with authority make the best candidates; people will not vote otherwise. Those are the tough guys, you know, with long sentences. Everyone listens to them."

Kevin Reilly entered the room, a gigantic keychain dangling from his belt. Joe and his team jumped into action, ushering everyone to their seats at the table. The prisoners, for their part, looked nervous. One of them, Ray, had told me earlier that he wanted to do right by the other prisoners who had entrusted this mission to them. Kevin Reilly reminded the group of the rules for this meeting. I noticed his body language: he was relaxed. After a round of introductions, it was Ray's turn to present his request. "Many of the phones in the common areas are broken," Ray said. "We get long queues and people start worrying that they might miss their turn. We want to call family, girlfriends, lawyers. It is important to us. Fights break out all the time over how long someone speaks on the phone. We end up hurting one another." Kevin Reilly repeated the request in his own words, promising to duly consider each request before the next session. Just before Ray was led out of the room, I asked him how it went. "I didn't mess up. I feel heard; I feel respected," he said. "Let's hope the governor gets some things done."

After the meeting of the prison council, as I made my way back down The Cally, I couldn't help but admire the genius of User Voice. It is one thing to figure that the governor and the prisoners should talk. But as ex-offenders, they also knew how hard it would be to actually have this conversation. Mark knew from experience how intimidating it is for prisoners to speak to the authorities. Probation officers, prison wardens, governors, or judges wield enormous power over their lives. And the stakes are even higher when addiction, mental health, money, and family problems come into play. Fearing repercussions, prisoners and ex-offenders often stay quiet even if they need help. And without their participation, the authorities have too little information to support their rehabilitation. It is a vicious circle marked by fear and distrust that frustrates everyone. User Voice filled a need no one else saw. And independent evaluations proved that these prison councils work.[2]

Prisoners across the UK open up to the people at User Voice who have lived through similar experiences. In 2009, when Mark Johnson founded the organization, no one had ever really involved users of probation services to improve outcomes. Between 2015 and 2021, User Voice has helped 127,000 ex-offenders take an active role in their probation. They recruited and trained more than fourteen hundred elected representatives to prison councils, where they developed four hundred service improvements. And 90 percent of prison officials agreed that this empowerment has benefited probation outcomes.[3] User Voice teaches us how we can slow down to listen, even within the urgency of an overcrowded prison. And they show us what it takes to do it right.

What's Your Favorite Color? Blue or Blue?

In the previous chapter, I shared my conversation with Georg about what really happened when our beautiful dinner party unraveled after our daughters talked about Fridays for Future. Put on the spot, Georg couldn't help but rush to restore order, even when he knew it was wrong. This experience made me look at my relationship to my own daughters in a new light. Am I the prison governor in their young lives? And if I am, have I come around to truly listening to them, like Kevin Reilly did in Pentonville Prison? Inspired by what I had learned from User Voice, I began to question my questions. What I learned is just how easy it is to disguise our fears and needs for control and domination as acts of listening. It was the "Saturday Question" that brought it all home for me.

The Fraught Saturday Question

Most Saturday mornings I asked my daughters what they would like to plan for the day. And instead of answering, they rolled their eyes. I, in turn, would be quietly (but visibly) annoyed. They, in turn, would wait for me to grudgingly leave them alone. But when their friends asked them the same question, I heard them answer with plenty of chatter and joy. What was going on here? User Voice had given me a new perspective to find out. Prison officials couldn't listen to prisoners because they were too afraid to speak openly to authorities with complete power over their lives. Something about the way my daughters rolled their eyes reminded me of prisoners avoiding answers to questions from probation officers. In prison, and as ex-offenders outside, they felt it was too risky to share difficult truths with people who wielded so much power over them. Was it possible that the same thing I observed in a prison played out in my home?

Rolling their eyes, I realized, was the only answer they could give. My daughters knew that my question was insincere long before I did. Had I not, over time, loaded my seemingly innocent question with unspoken expectations? We all knew that I wasn't open to whatever they might say. Instead, I wanted them to propose something meaningful. "Meaningful," by my definition, meant going to a museum, an exhibition, a walk, a hike, make or build something, draw or paint together. Answering my question carried an explosive risk because I was their father and held so much power over them. From the perspective of a child, was their fear of not meeting my expectations really so different from the fear prisoners experience about answering questions by prison authorities?

The truth was, this question—asked by me—was no more than a thinly veiled threat. And it did nothing to build their confidence, empower them, or build trust among us.

Why Is Good Listening So Hard?

I could just as well have asked "What's your favorite color? But it has to be blue." What shocked me most was that I hadn't realized how dishonest and manipulative my question was. The Saturday Question did nothing to achieve what I really want for my daughters: to empower them, to trust me, to share openly.

Why is good listening so hard? Listening was a challenge for me, not just at home. I struggled to get good answers from my colleagues, mentors, funders, and clients. They didn't roll their eyes, but I often felt dissatisfied with their responses. I would get confirmation of my opinions, but nothing new ever seemed to emerge. I began to think that I was the only smart person around. And I began to judge people, very smart people, for simply not giving me what I wanted.

At one point my fabulous coach Jan Weetjens observed: "Sascha, it is not really asking a question if you already provide the answer. To ask a question requires a complete openness to whatever you get. You don't get that by saying 'We have to do either A or B, and you must tell me by tomorrow!' Such a question reveals one of two things. Either how little faith you have in others, or how scared you are of their ideas. Keep asking this type of question, and those around you will lose their trust in giving you honest answers." This was a shocking observation. It was also great advice because I wanted to get good answers.

Show Me You're Listening!

How we listen reveals a lot about our intentions. An engineer at Facebook listens not to help people, but to manipulate them. User Voice practices a different form of listening, one with the goal of empowering prisoners to improve their rehabilitation process. And I, despite my best intentions, practiced my Saturday Question in a way that revealed my desire for control, thinly disguised as an open question.

I write about my family life not because it is interesting, but because our homes are a powerful mirror of the challenges we face in reconciling our desire for a Slow Lane world, with the false sense of security provided by the Fast Lane. We gravitate toward power and dominance because they seem such safe bets. If you attain power, you have a greater chance of bending reality to your liking, to your vision of the future. The danger, of course, lies in the inherent contradiction of how the singular vision of a leader like Elon Musk comes about when compared with the inclusive problem-solving practiced by User Voice. My Saturday Question tells us a lot about my vision for the future of my daughters, and what activities I consider to be meaningful ways to get there. The problem is, of course, that I also want them to be empowered to chart their own course, to act freely, and feel unconditionally loved and supported in whatever it is they do. There is just no way I can have it both ways.

How Much Trust Is in Your Listening?

If you want to stop pretending, listening comes down to being honest and intentional about two questions: (1) How far are you willing to trust others to know what is right? And (2) how honest are you with yourself about whether you believe that you are superior in your vision or ability to make that judgment? The Slow Lane has helped me interrogate my actions to reveal my intentions. It was a painful process because it revealed my hidden fears. At the same time, it was liberating. If the governor of a notorious prison can listen, so can I.

In his book *Theory U*, the MIT scholar C. Otto Scharmer identifies four levels of listening.[4] I think they are wonderful and align very well with what the Slow Lane teaches us about developing imagination in groups. The Slow Lane adds a dimension, by also highlighting the power dynamics at play.

- *"Yeah, I know that already." Downloading.* Listening for what you want to hear, confirming your opinions. This is me asking my daughters what they would like to do on a Saturday. But in the context of my power over them, it is barely a question because not only am I listening for what

I would like to hear, but I also let them feel that I judge all else.

- *"Ooh, look at that!"* *Factual.* This is gathering information, even if it contradicts what you know. It is sensing, collecting data, testing. Many companies and governments do this when they run surveys, ask for feedback, collect ideas. The listening is strictly on the terms of the listener—but inviting new information to come forward. It is an essential way of gathering data, piecing together a better picture of the situation.

- *"Oh yes, I know how you feel."* *Empathy.* Here, as a listener, we begin to notice a shift away from our point of view, or from simply gathering facts, to seeing the world through the eyes of others. This kind of listening let Kevin Reilly take the point of view of the prisoners to see how even small technical problems like broken phones caused a spiral of personal anxiety that led to violence in the prison. It can signal a shift of power.

- *"I can't express what I experience in words. My whole being has slowed down. I am connected to something larger than myself."* *Generative.* This is the most advanced form of listening, the place where together we imagine something new. In our stories this generative listening is deeply rooted in the practice of building, empowering, and serving a community. Here the listener opens up to something entirely new, leading to transformative visions for change.

A Few Honest Changes

Once I realized how fraught my Saturday Question was, I began to change things. The first thing I did was to speak openly with my daughters about what I learned. How, subconsciously, I had used this question to exert power over them. They both laughed with relief, happy that it was out in the open. I have tried to be more honest about my questions ever since. For example, a few months into the pandemic we decided to leave New York City and move abroad. Julia and I decided to do things differently this time, giving our daughters more of a say. Our last move had been from Barcelona to New York, and at the time we mostly sold the decision to our daughters.

Asked about it, Olivia said, "You told me that it would only be for two years, at most. That wasn't true!" And she was right, that's precisely what we had done. So this time we informed them that we would have to leave New York, but that we didn't know where we would end up. Our commitment was this: we will be 100 percent honest with you, share all information, and you will have a say about where we end up. Together, our family took eight months to figure this out. Then we moved to Berlin.

I asked my daughters if they felt that anything had changed since I came to see the Saturday Question in a new light. Sofía said, "Yes, you became more open. Now, we can sometimes do nothing more than go for ice cream. These days, when you ask, I know it is an invitation more than a trick question. I can choose to tag along, or do something else. I can be honest in my reply. And it made all of us a bit more independent." When it came to our move to Berlin, Sofía felt included, that we made decisions together.

Olivia saw a similar change, feeling less worried about having to say what I want to hear. She sometimes still feels a bit pressured when I ask the Saturday Question, but she says that's more because she doesn't know what she wants herself. And even in those moments she feels that I understand and accept her more openly than before. The days when my daughters felt pressured to go to a museum seem over. Olivia did point out, though, that all wasn't perfect—she remains acutely aware of how even if I am more honest, there are still moments when she can sense that she is being manipulated. Like when she senses that I present her mostly with information that supports my preferred outcome. After reading George Orwell, she now calls those the "1984 moments" in our relationship.

In the end it is our most personal relationships that reveal how hard it is to change our ways. Everything inside and around us seems to nudge us to pretend and to discourage real listening. Even our unknown fears push us to the apparent safety of exerting control. And yet we know that dominance will not actually lead to a better future because it disenfranchises those we want to protect the most. These are uncomfortable truths, for any person, parent, member of a community, or leader. But I found the answers to be surprisingly simple, especially once I faced my fears and resolved to trust those around me.

The Slow Lane Government

I seem to smell the stench of appeasement in the air.

Margaret Thatcher

The Slow Lane is for governments too.[5] Sefton, a city of 275,000 on the outskirts of Liverpool in England, was already stumbling when, after decades of decline, the 2007–2008 financial crisis hit. The city council budget was cut in half in 2012, just when people needed help the most. At that point, city leaders took an unusual turn: instead of imposing cuts from above, they involved citizens at every step of the way to become part of the solution. Sefton became a listening government.

That year, Peter Moore received an unpleasant assignment, the one that nobody working in a local government wants. He was a social service commissioner in Sefton. Among the many cutbacks, city leaders had determined that they could no longer afford to provide the community meals service, which brought hot meals to 350 of the city's most vulnerable, mainly elderly, people. The program cost the city about $300,000 a year. Peter Moore had to cut that cost to zero.

Left Behind by the Fast Lane for Fifty Years

Many families in Sefton had already fallen on really hard times following years of industrial decline. Sefton used to be a rich place with a big industrial port, much like Hamburg, where I come from. As I walked through Sefton, I saw landmarks of splendor, like Sefton Park Palm House, gifted by a local millionaire in the 1870s. I also saw the docks, where most of the workers, often fathers and sons, had earned their living for generations and created the city's wealth. Sefton clearly had been a thriving community.

To the people of Sefton, the port means more than work. It is part of the soul of the community. The docks even produced a local language: Scouse, the local dialect, arose from the melting pot of local dockworkers and sailors from around the world. But starting in the 1970s, slowly at first, the port lost its importance. Jobs were cut and unemployment rose. In an attempt to make the economy more competitive, Margaret Thatcher, the prime minister, fought the dockworkers' unions to free businesses from having to deal with workers they no longer needed. Families lost their income, and young people their job prospects. In 1981, in nearby Toxteth, thousands of desperate people protested and rioted against racism and poverty. Thatcher wanted to put the economy firmly into the Fast Lane of globalization, and her advisers told her to just let the region decline.[6]

I first visited Sefton in 1996 as a student, spending time at the picket line with the last unionized dockworkers. They were on strike in solidarity over the lack of job prospects for their sons. Many families in Sefton were the problem left behind. By 2012, when Peter Moore took on the job of cutting the funds that delivered food to 350 of the most vulnerable households, things again looked dire. Not only had Sefton families lived through forty years of decline, but now the global financial crisis had hit them as well. Once again, families in Sefton found themselves suffering from a major global event that they had nothing to do with. The docks had long gone, and unemployment was high. In 2010, in response to the financial crisis, the conservative prime minister David Cameron announced years of austerity measures for the country.[7] Austerity means spending less on government services. In Sefton it meant cutting half the city budget, or about $300 million, at a time when half the children in some neighborhoods (and 25 percent on average across the city) lived in poverty. Community meals was just one of many services on the line.

How to Flip a Job from Hell

I don't envy Peter Moore for his assignment. As it was, Sefton could already no longer keep up with helping families in need. Child poverty, poor health, and unemployment were rising fast. Many families had to make very tough choices, like choosing between buying food or heating their homes in winter. And here he was, tasked with cutting the spending on hot meals for some of the hardest hit. But he took an optimistic approach. What if, by listening closely, he could find a way to not let people down?

Here is how Sefton's community meals worked. People who needed meals had to pay $5 per meal to the city. The city had hired a food company to provide those meals, paying an additional $3 to subsidize the meal. In all, this amounted to a $300,000 annual government subsidy. Under normal circumstances Peter might have rebalanced the budget, but this was no longer an option. He would have to completely cut the $300,000 subsidy. He asked a more basic question: What was it that people using the program really need? To find out, he asked local volunteers to meet community meals users in their homes. They talked not just about meals, but about their needs more broadly. One thing he learned was that nobody much liked the food they were getting through the program. Everyone got the same meal, every day. Another thing they learned was that people were lonely. For many, the meal delivery was the only human contact they had in a day, and they were afraid of losing it. In other words, community meals were about much more than providing food.

Peter set out to solve each of the needs. To tackle the loneliness issue, Peter partnered with the charity Age Concern. They now coordinated their volunteers to visit the users of community meals, to listen properly, and to connect them with activities in the city like cycling or walking groups, social services, or help with managing money. To address the food deliveries, Peter, and his team, got help from local food businesses. Forty of them agreed to provide hot meals at the same $5 out-of-pocket cost to residents but without the $3 government subsidy. That ended up giving people more choice, to select meals from dozens of menus instead of getting the same old meal each day. By the time Peter was done, he had not only saved Sefton the $300,000. He had also found a better way to meet his residents' needs.

Sharing the Ability to Fix the City

Paul Cummins, a city councilor and Peter's boss at the time, was the political leader responsible for social services. For more than ten years, in an effort to find $300 million in budget savings, Paul and his team applied the same tactics of involving residents at every step to find creative solutions. This way of empowering people gradually changed the way the whole city government worked.

Like when Sefton had to cut 20 percent from its $24 million budget for supported living—a program that provides cooking, cleaning, shopping, and personal finance support to people with special needs. They brought both care providers and users into the process. Following the community meals method, they focused not just on spending cuts but created a shared vision of what actually mattered most for residents' independence. Sefton groomed local nonprofits so that they would be ready to compete for public contracts against the corporate providers the city had used in the past, to have more caring partners from within the community.

In 2020, I asked Paul what this intense period felt like to him. "My party, the Labour Party, took over Sefton City Council in 2012," he recalled. "Politically, we were opposed to the central government's austerity campaign, which had painted local governments like Sefton as lazy and wasteful. It was a political nightmare. And a moral nightmare because so many people were suffering. But we took that frustration and turned it into a mission to invest ourselves in making the best of a situation we knew we could not control." Peter added: "It was really exhausting work, we were all pushed to our limits. Especially because we had to be creative whilst carrying so much responsibility for vulnerable people."

Frustration turned into a mission: Sefton's leaders invested themselves in making the best of a situation they could not control. They became a listening government.

Winning as a Slow Lane Government...

Paul's party got reelected, despite cutting so many services. Voters bought into the new model of being honest about the hard realities and involving people in implementing cuts. Paul said that "none of this would have been possible without the voluntary organizations in Sefton. We realized, much like Peter did with the community meals, that these organizations are very close to the people who need support and best understand their needs." He continued: "At first, we did budget cuts the old 'patriarchal' way. What I mean is that we, the public leaders, sat down and decided what to cut. That's how government used to work, it was part of the power we held. But the crisis forced us to change that quickly. We began to work with everyone to make sure that we would put the little money we had to good use. And it completely changed how the city now does its business, how the whole government works."

Facing their most dire crisis, leaders in Sefton turned to listening. Giving up power as a government, what Paul Cummins called "the old patriarchal way" is one of the hardest transitions to make. Most cities, including progressive cities like Santa Monica, California, simply imposed brutal cuts following the financial crisis and again later when Covid-19 hit.[8] Sefton's leaders realized that they could no longer depend on the usual "citizen consultation," simply asking people to nod off their proposals. Instead, Sefton had to trust the people it was supposed to serve to carry part of the responsibility. Even the most disadvantaged groups had valuable contributions to make—as experts in their lives, they helped prioritize what mattered most. Sefton turned to citizens and volunteers to listen to people at an unprecedented scale. With it, Sefton's leaders shifted power and control to the community, as it did with community meals and the supported living services now run by local nonprofits who co-designed the service.

...Means Stepping Out of the Fast Lane

The Fast Lane proved an unreliable partner to Sefton. In the decades running up to the financial crisis, Sefton, like most other cities, had outsourced most of its services to corporations. People believed that the private sector and market competition would be more innovative and efficient. But as Sefton's needs changed during the crisis years, companies turned their backs on community needs, rigidly sticking to what was written into their precrisis contracts. Following this experience, Sefton began to think more carefully about whom to do business with. If the key to getting through hard times is listening and learning from people, governments should have partners who do just that. It sought out local community-led organizations and businesses that share Sefton's values and taught them how to win the business of caring for the city.

Make Trust the New Black

Listening in the Slow Lane is a way to share power with the people who suffer the consequences our quick fixes create. Good listening starts with seeing our listening theater for what it is. Whether at home, in movements, in business, or in government, we are (often unwitting) experts at pretending to listen to those around us. Instead of waiting to have our hands forced by a painful crisis like leaders in Sefton did, we can acknowledge these shortcomings and start listening.

I feel fortunate to have seen these great listeners in action for years. I know what good listening looks like. Still, in practice I keep falling back into what experts call tokenism, or pretending to listen. It is simply too easy to act like I am listening. My Saturday Question was just a thinly veiled game of power. To stop pretending, I have to keep returning to find my answer to the two questions that help us reveal our true intentions: (1) How far am I willing to trust others to know what is right? And (2) How superior am I in my vision or ability to make that judgment?

The Listening Theater

Most stories in this book start in a place where powerful people or institutions engage in the theater of listening. It is a quick

fix. Sefton did a lot of "listening" in the form of the generic
public consultation efforts, sending out a survey or asking people for feedback on a planned project. And Pentonville Prison,
just like the UK Probation Services, asked people about their
rehabilitation needs under conditions that made it impossible
to speak the truth. Like my Saturday Question, these activities looked like listening but were ineffective in creating real
change.

There is an interesting parallel here to what psychologists
found out about human communications. What we say is just
40 percent of the message we convey, the rest comes in the form
of gestures, posture, expressions, and context. All of these are
called nonverbal communication. Psychologists have observed
that it is easy to pretend in the words we say but much harder
to pretend in what our body language communicates as we say
it. In listening, the same holds true. There is only so much pretending we can do without really meaning it. And really meaning it, when it comes to listening, comes down to unconditional
trust. That's the really hard nut to crack.

A Good Crisis Builds Trust

At home I found it very difficult to ask an honest question without resolving the trust issue. Do I trust my daughters to know
what is right? What if they choose to do none of the activities
that I find meaningful? It wasn't until I let go of my plans for
their future that I could really ask an honest question. That's
definitely like opening a can of worms: Would they have a
future, if I let go? What would others think? How would I be
judged by family and friends? Would they embarrass me by
not adhering to my definition of success in life? Would they
suffer painful setbacks in life? My desire to protect them by
controlling them directly contradicted my even greater desire
to empower them, to give them agency over their lives.

Could I unconditionally love my children, without trusting them unconditionally? Unlearning my instincts and justifications for being the "benevolent dictator" in their lives didn't come easy. My personal struggles are really no different from what defines the stories throughout this book. People and institutions in power eventually come around to trusting people who aren't supposed to be competent: our children and youth, women, the poor, the uneducated, offenders and ex-offenders, nonexperts, ordinary citizens. Choosing trust feels very counterintuitive. It rarely stands a chance against the predictability of exerting power.

We are taught that great leaders are made in a crisis. They look after us, they place all the right bets, rally the troops, and quickly issue instructions. Leading this way also feels like a natural act of self-preservation: if I am in charge, I have control over my fate. Picking the path of power and dominance is particularly attractive when we feel cornered into believing that we need a simple quick fix that will set us free. Think about it: Sefton had to cut 50 percent of its spending right away, and Pentonville Prison was drowning in violence. In these situations our instincts tell us that listening is just a slow way to get a lot of confusing input, when all you want is a simple fix.

Finding the "Always" in the Crisis

If opting for listening is so counterintuitive, why have people in our stories decided to do it? They had simply come to the end of the line. Their quick fixes were becoming less and less effective at getting them out of trouble. And so, they had to take a longer view. The turning points in these stories may seem like moments of acute crisis, a shock to the system, but they really are about chronic problems. Pentonville had been spiraling out of control for generations. Sefton had been declining for decades. And every Saturday, I got absolutely nowhere.

Stepping back, reassessing, and arriving at a new perspective. This kind of reframing allows us to step out of the hamster wheel of hobbling from crisis to crisis, the moment when we see the bigger picture. Sefton realized that it didn't urgently need to cut its budget, but that it was always so vulnerable to outside forces that it couldn't reliably serve its people. And Kevin Reilly, the governor of Pentonville Prison, realized that for 172 years leaders like himself always implemented quick fixes that in the end failed to help people rehabilitate and return to society.

The Fast Lane perpetuates this "always" in our crises, since the quick fixes only ever work for some people. Over time, the rest become silent and invisible because they are so tied up in the difficulties these quick fixes create for them. It is a vicious and inhumane circle. People become the inconvenient truth we look away from. With time, they become too exhausted to make themselves heard. You can see where this is going: the more we fix things the Fast Lane way, the more we feed the downward spiral for those left behind, driving a deeper wedge between us and them. The numbers of those left behind can be staggering: 25 percent of children grow up impoverished in Sefton, 40 percent do in Spain.

Listening in the Slow Lane, however, shifts real power to people who were always excluded from the quick fixes and tied up in the side effects.

Permanent, Open, Patient, Generous, Giving

Will it always take a crisis to push us to listen properly? There are two ways to look at this question. The first response is a simple no, since we are free to listen whenever we want. A longer answer starts with a yes, simply because we actually live in a permanent crisis, made up of slow-moving "always" problems, like climate change, social injustice, broken systems, and inequality. Shocks like the financial crisis or the Covid-19 pandemic end up revealing these "always" problems. Care workers had been reduced to disposable, low-cost labor long before the pandemic. Covid-19 simply made everyone take notice of how critical their role is—and how poorly rewarded they are. This is what people mean when they talk about systemic change: to not shy away from listening to where it hurts most.

How to Make Trust the New Black

Here are some ideas on what we can do, right now, to listen better.

Each one of us can do more, every day, to break out of our hamster wheel. Take a moment every time you find yourself justifying that it is okay to put yourself above others—be they your loved ones or otherwise. Don't wait for a crisis; instead, take courage from knowing that trusting others will let them thrive and contribute. Doing this is hard, especially in a Fast Lane world that promises salvation and safety to those in charge.

We can also organize to be listened to. Mark Johnson was an offender and prisoner before he started User Voice to give ex-offenders a voice. His group demanded a say and, in doing so, taught society how the incarcerated and ex-offenders can be heard and treated with dignity. People like Kevin Reilly supported them. Here, too, change started from within: they had to unlearn their ways to put themselves at the service of those who had never wielded power.

In business we can start by being honest with ourselves about our own listening. Is listening a tool for us to exploit our customers and partners? Or are we listening to give them a real say? Can we reconcile our business model with good listening, and what would that mean for our sustainability and growth? These questions aren't cosmetic; rather, they go straight to the heart of why you started a business in the first place. Can the stories in this chapter inspire you to change things?

And governments can listen too. Sefton has shown how even powerful government institutions can create an environment of trust. This isn't new. It is at the heart of what is called Asset-Based Community Development (ABCD), a sustainable development methodology developed in the early 1990s.[9] With ABCD, communities invest in the abilities of people, instead of seeing them as problems. Sefton, in the past, viewed citizens as needs to be serviced. Now, Sefton sees citizens for their ability to contribute.

Governments can change, but this transition is hard for them too. Two changes would start to make a real difference. The first is to give enough space, time, and support to ensure that all kinds of citizens can find their voice, instead of demanding answers to fit a bureaucratic timetable. Remember how prisoners spent several months with the team of User Voice to prepare for their first meeting with the governor? You simply can't force empowerment. The second change is to give people as much control as possible over decisions that affect their lives. This can play out in different ways. Officials won't let prisoners take charge of running their prison, but considering their proposals can go a long way. Sefton, for instance, can let citizens decide what support they want to live independently.

Listening that is free from fear opens a whole new world of care, dignity, and creativity. It creates a world in which instead of imposing our answers on others, we invite people in to develop their own.

= 3 =

Share the Agency

A hero (heroine in its feminine form) is a real person
or a main fictional character who, in the face of danger,
combats adversity through feats of ingenuity, courage,
or strength.

"Hero" as defined by Wikipedia

Who should be in charge? The Fast Lane answer is "the best
person." A leader of exceptional skill and quality, a visionary,
someone who can channel the complexity of the world into a
determined set of actions. Someone willing to take risks. And
how do we find such a person? They come out on top because
the best people, whether in competitive politics or business,
come out on top. By this logic the Fast Lane justifies that a
single person (or small group) takes charge.

This is how powerful people end up imposing their solutions on the rest. Or, put differently: if you have succeeded in
the Fast Lane, you have accumulated the power to impose your
solution on others. It is by this logic that political leaders in
Spain justified the "bitter medicine," the severe financial austerity measures that ruined the lives of millions of people. Had
they not come out on top in competitive elections? Had they not

been advised by finance experts, economists, and other countries who had all come out on top? To Fast Lane leaders, listening or even involving ordinary people is a very slow way to get confusing input from people who cannot grasp the complexity of the decision at hand.

It is also true that we live in a world in which very few of the leaders who impose solutions actually succeed. Millions of Spaniards who suffered the bitter medicine voted with their feet: they upended the political establishment and gave rise to new grassroots political movements in a hope to get a say in future decisions. The rise of the Green Party in Germany is testament to a similar dynamic. Mistaking themselves for great leaders, the political establishment at the time dismissed farmers, families, and environmentalists as incompetent on the matter of energy. In this instance, too, ordinary people voted with their feet and created a powerful political alternative.

This chapter explores how the Slow Lane shares the agency, instead of imposing solutions. Instead of betting on singular genius, successful Slow Lane movements create pathways for even the least prepared or informed people to join the efforts toward change. Our first story unfolds in Zalău, a provincial town in Romania. "Caring for One Is Caring for a Million," begins when eighteen-year-old Oana is diagnosed with a disease unknown to medical professionals in Romania. Her mother, Dorica Dan, started a movement around this disease of one. Twenty years later, rare disease patients like Oana have created a new way of providing health care for all. And they have taken a full seat on the national council that oversees Romania's health-care reform.

From small-town Romania we move on to Peru. In "How Albina Shook Up a Country by Listening to Its Waste," we follow the story of Albina Ruiz and her movement that empowered hundreds of thousands of waste-pickers. They went on to become respected recycling professionals, protected by law, putting their country on track to become a zero-waste economy. The last story in this chapter, "Solving For, Solving With," takes us to New York City. Rosanne Haggerty pioneered a new model of supported living that helped homeless and HIV-positive people rebuild their lives in dignity. From there, she launched a bold national campaign to end homelessness that is racking up successes. Meanwhile, in Brownsville, New York City, Rosanne's organization has started a program to ensure racial equity, putting families in charge of what it's like to grow up in their neighborhood.

These stories are uniquely powerful in countering the Fast Lane belief that only a genius, a heroic leader, can be truly visionary. Dorica, Albina, and Rosanne teach us the opposite. Instead of putting the brakes on transformative ideas for the future, enabling others to be part of the solution can lead to even more audacious ideas. Ideas that become real. Empowering people with rare diseases to rebuild the health-care system is revolutionary. Empowering waste-pickers, long stigmatized, discarded, and persecuted, to become the heroes of a sustainable waste and recycling economy is transformative. And so is ending homelessness and letting families right the wrongs of systemic racism to rebuild their social services. In short, the Slow Lane accomplishes what the Fast Lane has been unable to deliver: solving the "always" problems.

The Slow Lane empowers everyone to lead. Sharing the agency starts with being of service. Empathy and care build deep and trusting relationships, providing the stability people need to contribute according to their full abilities. The truly audacious ideas emerge, and become real, when we offer the time and space for others to get involved in finding new answers.

Caring for One Is Caring for a Million

Olga Shirobokova told me that I really ought to talk to Dorica Dan. Olga and I were collaborating on a podcast series for Ashoka, exchanging stories about people who did extraordinary work with governments. Dorica was, it turned out, doing much more than that. She was a sophisticated practitioner of sharing the agency. A Zoom call brought me into Dorica's home in Romania in the late summer of 2020.

Here is what you need to know about Dorica: She grew up in the late 1960s in a remote area of Romania, contracting polio at the age of five. As a result, she had to spend a lot of time far away from her family, in one of just two treatment centers in Romania. As a student in the early 1980s, Dorica gave birth to her daughter Oana. Something was wrong—Oana wasn't eating or crying. Doctors couldn't diagnose her. She had a rare disease, unknown to Romanian medical professionals. Having suffered a complex and rare disease herself, Dorica decided to stop her studies to support her daughter. For a while, she volunteered in the classroom to help her daughter integrate. Years later, in 2003, when Oana was eighteen, she finally received a diagnosis in Italy: Oana had the rare Prader-Willi syndrome. A disease with no other known cases among Romania's population of twenty-two million people.

The Movement of One

With Oana being the only known person in Romania diagnosed with Prader-Willi syndrome, it seemed like a strange move for Dorica to establish the Romanian Prader-Willi Association. It had just three members: Oana, Dorica, and her husband, who himself also suffered a rare disease. They traveled to international conferences to build a network of global experts and organized the first-ever Prader-Willi syndrome conference in

Romania to build awareness and get attention from medical professionals. Hardly anyone attended the conference, but leaflets circulated and some people began to reach out. Dorica's prior work with a disability organization helped her gain some trust from people in the Romanian ministry of health. But the corridors of power were far away, with Dorica's family living in Zalău, a remote town in a poor part of the country.

The family's lived experience with rare diseases gave Dorica a deep sense of what was needed. As she researched treatments, she mostly found medical answers to a condition that involved many other factors. They had seen what it took for Oana to thrive, to overcome physical and social barriers. Success in managing the disease was impossible unless you worked very closely with the patient, and everyone around her.

That, it turned out, was a need of not just one, but many.

The Movement of Ones

Oana may have been the only known case of Prader-Willi in Romania, but many other people suffered from other rare diseases. A rare disease is a disorder that affects fewer than one in two thousand people, resulting in little attention by doctors, researchers, and the pharmaceutical industry. This lack of demand leaves most rare diseases without treatment, makes available treatments incredibly expensive and specialists scarce. There are an estimated ten thousand such rare diseases.[1] Everyone who suffered one of these conditions in Romania was likely to share Oana's experience of being undiagnosed, untreated, excluded, and afraid. The health system didn't meet their needs. Dorica began to think differently about her cause. What if they could build a health system that works for all people with rare diseases? And what if they could offer a welcoming place for them to get help, near to where they live?

In a country of twenty-two million a disease of one couldn't be heard. By reframing the story, Dorica made it an urgent national issue. That reframing brought a new sense of scale to the situation. More than a million people, or 6 percent of the population of Romania, suffer from rare diseases. At least 95 percent of them had yet to be diagnosed, meaning that they had no access to treatment. Most patients didn't even know they had a rare disease. It took Dorica's family eighteen years, and international contacts, to get Oana diagnosed. The fact that she was the first one in Romania spoke volumes. Statistically, there should have been a thousand just like her.

What more than a million people had in common with Oana was that they were left behind by a system that caters only to the big diseases. A health system that works for people with rare diseases would have to be different, able to respond to a million uncommon needs. To put this concern on the map, Dorica brought the international Prader-Willi conference to Romania in 2007, attracting experts and delegates from around the world. That same year, to unite the field, she founded the National Alliance for Rare Diseases, joining forces with thirty-eight other patient organizations and influential doctors. Together, this alliance began to develop a national plan for rare diseases.

Building Rare Infrastructure

Dorica and her fellow activists looked for creative ways to make headway. After all, at this point in Romania only a few thousand people knew they suffered a rare disease. The vast majority still had no idea. The alliance's vision was simple and inclusive: all people should have access to diagnosis and the necessary kind of care. For people with rare diseases, this required a new approach. Care would have to be holistic to include all aspects of life, and patients would need to actively participate. To many medical professionals and policy makers, however, this was counterintuitive, as they saw themselves as experts administering drugs and developing medical treatment plans.

In 2011, Dorica opened NoRo, the first reference center in Europe for people with rare diseases, run by people with rare diseases. From the outset NoRo offered information and special services all in one place. Social services, training in disease management and independent living, support in the education system and finding a job. The goal: to empower individuals with rare diseases to thrive in society. Compared to the national scale at which the coalition developed plans, NoRo was tiny. And deep. In Dorica's mind, this was no contradiction. Patients needed good, holistic services. These in turn strengthened connections among patients, organizing them into a community. NoRo began training thousands of medical professionals, to improve care and form a national referral network. NoRo's helpline helped thousands of people by connecting them to medical professionals, care offerings, and other patients. By offering a high-quality, compassionate service, Dorica offered a place people would turn to. That in turn helped grow their national movement.

And NoRo is only a prototype. Dorica and her team are working toward a national network of one-stop-shop care facilities for people diagnosed with rare diseases. It is a living example of how a future health system for rare diseases in Romania could work. NoRo, for example, offers volunteering experiences that build bridges between the local community and patients. Taken together, Dorica is building a very cost-effective, highly personalized infrastructure that welcomes people who don't fit into existing systems of care.

Building a Care System, within a Health-Care System

NoRo was never going to be enough to change the entire health-care system. It offered a point of reference, but it was the national plan for rare diseases that brought decision makers to the table. In Romania, like elsewhere, this is a complex process. They needed to win over the national ministry of health to fund new treatments. Other ministries were needed to recognize the needs of people with rare diseases in education, employment, and housing. Local governments had to change the way they provided services. Paying for such a plan is complex. To get NoRo off the ground, Dorica pieced together a partnership between the government of Norway, the local government of Zalău, and the Romanian Prader-Willi association.

Dorica and her team soon noticed how hard it was to keep everyone's eye on the prize. Large bureaucracies can get caught up in their own workings, losing focus on helping rare disease patients. Things moved slowly. One way Dorica's movement sought to maintain focus was to promote media coverage. The team trained journalists to become public storytellers, creating the School of Journalists on Rare Diseases. By 2020 more than two hundred journalists had received the training, reporting stories about the disease, celebrating leaders who take action, and following up on progress. An annual journalism award celebrates the best stories.

Power to the Patients!

A major breakthrough occurred in 2014, when the Romanian government approved the national rare disease plan and formed a national council to oversee the implementation. Rare disease patients got seats on this council, with voting rights. It was a big win, after a frustrating six years, in which the government seemed to stall. Romania became only the second country in Europe to implement a rare disease strategy.

When Dorica talks about her movement, she actually talks about transforming the whole health-care system. According to her, more and more health treatments will be tailored to people's individual needs, requiring the kind of approaches that already help patients of rare diseases today. The current model of medicine is not just ineffective but also wasteful. Not responding to patients holistically creates a lot of waste between health and other social services. Focusing on rare diseases, NoRo has already run dozens of innovative programs. They trained health professionals, adapted new technologies to local needs, influenced European policy, and deployed online care offerings during the Covid-19 pandemic. In addition to being a community and service center, NoRo has become a lab that translates the latest global ideas into Romania's new health-care model.

By putting patients in charge, NoRo does what many Slow Lane movements do so well: they listen for the changing needs of people by being of service. NoRo excels at responding to a patient's individual needs, medical and otherwise. From the perspective of scale, it is a true one-to-one operation. This, Dorica tells me, is the secret sauce. It gives patients the strength, and confidence, to take agency and help each other. And represent themselves in the national rare disease council, to make better decisions for a million people.

Jumping Scales

Dorica is a masterful operator of scale, showing how we can share the agency at the one-to-one level and change a national system. She focuses on what all patients have in common. She found that what works for Oana works for other individuals with rare diseases. This, in turn, will work for all. Dorica's approach is simple: listen to patients as whole people, tailor services to the scale of one, empower patients to contribute to the system. Sharing the agency in this way allowed the movement to succeed. It inspired everyone involved to imagine ever more transformative change, and to bring it within reach.

How Albina Shook Up a Country
by Listening to Its Waste

Many Slow Lane movements start out by solving a specific local
problem that leads to an audacious vision for change. Shocked
by mountains of trash in the 1970s, Albina Ruiz set out to fix
a dysfunctional municipal waste collection system in a neighborhood of Lima, Peru's capital city. Over the course of four decades, her method of understanding the root causes, listening,
and empowering others has helped create a national movement
that transformed the lives of thousands of impoverished waste-
pickers. And set Peru on a path to becoming cleaner, healthier,
and more sustainable.

Stumbling into a Mountain of Trash

Take a deep breath. Imagine yourself in the Amazonian rainforest. The deep green, the rich smells and vegetation, the sounds.
This is where the Slow Lane journey of Albina Ruiz began. She
was sixteen when she left her home in Moyobamba, known as
the city of orchids in the Peruvian rainforest, to travel a thousand kilometers to Lima, Peru's capital city. It was 1976; she
wanted to study engineering. Albina's siblings already lived in
Lima and taught her about living in this city of over five million
people: how to use a bus, how to avoid trouble, and how to stay
safe by looking away when a crime is committed. They lived in
Villa El Salvador, one of the poor areas on the outskirts of the
city.

Villa El Salvador, at the time, was a slum. Albina saw giant
mountains of trash dumped all over her neighborhood. It was
a shocking experience, as there had been no waste heaps in
the jungle. Waste was managed poorly all over Peru. Quite
commonly, it was dumped in the poorest neighborhoods on the
outskirts of the cities. Albina tells me that at the time, public

leaders, including lecturers at her university, stigmatized the poor. One official told her: "Poor people won't mind the dirt because they are dirty themselves." And since poor people mostly didn't pay taxes, many officials thought that poor people didn't deserve proper municipal services. Across the country poor families lived among these rat-infested mountains of trash. And they lived off them, leaving their pigs to feed on scraps of waste. Thousands of people were waste-pickers, scouring these mountains to collect materials to sell. Eyed with suspicion, they were harassed and persecuted by police.

Listening for the Social Life of Trash

Albina completed her studies in industrial engineering and environmental management and went on to earn a PhD in chemistry. But already in her first years of engineering studies, on project placement in the municipal government of El Agustino, another poor neighborhood, her research revealed how broken the official waste collection system was. There was corruption everywhere. Like when companies sold fancy trucks to municipalities for a lot of money. They would give officials illegal kickbacks, cash as a reward for buying expensive machines. Albina saw that, to improve things, municipalities needed good people in waste management. People who were qualified and motivated. But instead, with the little money municipal leaders had left after buying costly vehicles, they hired unqualified people, mainly men, who didn't care for their communities and carried out their work poorly.

Waste in Peru was not just an environmental problem. It was a mirror of a broken society. Next to corruption, there was a lot of prejudice against poor people, especially waste-pickers. Albina told me that while the prejudice against poor people was that they were dirty, it was actually the rich who were dumping their waste everywhere, even out of the windows of their cars.

The difference, Albina recalls, was that in rich areas the streets would be cleaned. In the poor areas no one came to clean up. Letting poor people live among mountains of trash was just one of many insults they had to endure.

Shaking Up the Business

But to Albina, waste also had value. There was value in collecting waste, recycling it, and reusing the materials that could be extracted. She began to help people in areas like Villa El Salvador start microbusinesses to collect and treat waste. Many of these were started by women who were picking through waste for scraps. They created thousands of jobs and made their communities cleaner and healthier. Albina set up a local and then a national association of recyclers. Together, the association approached municipalities to offer their waste management services. Instead of expensive vehicles, they used simple tricycles. They offered no kickbacks but good waste management. Some recyclers went from earning three dollars a day to earning closer to fifteen dollars a day. Some families were able to save enough to send their children to university.

Edilberto Delgado has lived through this journey.[2] He became a recycler in Villa El Salvador when he was just six years old, starting to work at 5 a.m., alongside his mother, to beat the crowds on the waste dump. Fights broke out as waste-pickers raced to the fresh loads dumped by trucks. Later in the day, at school, Edilberto was bullied because of the smell that soap couldn't wash off his body. Growing up recycling, for him, was a shameful activity, the lowest job possible. Already as a small child, his self-esteem seemed to have hit rock-bottom. "We lived like rats," he says.

And yet, Edilberto and his mother were of immense service to the environment, recycling half a ton of plastic, carton, and paper every month. The system wasn't just dangerous and inhumane but also wildly inefficient. Edilberto remembers watching as tons of unrecycled waste were burned off and buried every week by official waste managers—long before the valuable materials could be extracted by recyclers. He stuck to recycling, and by the time he was eighteen, Edilberto had a family of his own and became part of a group who collected waste using tricycles, for about fifty cents a load. With no waste disposal facilities in the city, they would simply dump the waste in public gardens and parks. It was a shameful way to earn a living, dumping waste around the city, and the police were persecuting them. But Edilberto was providing for his family.

Things began to change when Edilberto learned about Albina's NGO, Ciudad Saludable. It offered paths to ecological recycling and better livelihoods. In return for training, uniforms, and support, Edilberto had to give up his illegal operations. Together with six other recyclers he formed an association, Acavida, and won municipal concessions to process about thirty tons of household and business waste every month. His team got access to a collection center and, thanks to Ciudad Saludable, obtained a $7,000 bank loan to buy a collection truck.

Everybody Statecraft to Change the Game

Stories like Edilberto's offered hope to Albina, proving that change was possible. At the same time, she felt overwhelmed by the scale of the problem: 87 percent of recyclers were still living in extreme poverty, and her life would be too short to solve this problem in Peru's eighteen hundred municipalities. Ciudad Saludable proved an important resource to municipalities and recyclers like Edilberto, and in 2000 the movement, backed by the NGO, decided to lobby the national government to write an employment law that would protect recyclers. After four years of lobbying, the government produced no more than an ineffective technical guide.

82

Learning from this setback, the movement set out to get a law passed again in 2007. This time, instead of just proposing a law behind closed doors, they organized a national movement and worked with people seconded from a variety of ministries, meeting several times a week. This time round they helped the recyclers themselves to take a seat at the negotiating table. Ciudad Saludable hired journalists to help them express their ideas clearly.

It worked. They reached a political tipping point when they had a draft law on the table, backed by positive results from using similar laws in seventy municipalities. Their collective effort proved that the 190,000 families working in recycling in Peru, constituting almost 2 percent of the national vote, could deliver significant cost savings and environmental benefits. To secure momentum at this critical point, recyclers from across the country organized a Happiness March on the capital. And this time they got what they wanted. In 2009, thirty-three years after Albina started this work, Peru was the first country in the world to pass a law to provide recyclers with health and employment protections.

A Law Is Nothing until We Make It Real

La Ley del Reciclador (the law of the recycler), as it is formally known, recognizes the work of recyclers as a job category.[3] They could no longer be legally exploited and were guaranteed safe working conditions and fair pay. Peru's ministry of health began offering recyclers universal access to health care and vaccination. Through local partners the government provided official training schemes, offered free of charge, to certify recyclers. The whole training program was tailored to the needs of people who experience extreme poverty, work long hours, and can't read or write.

The law was a great win, but the movement soon found that

a law alone would not be enough. Petitioned by recyclers, the government created incentives for municipalities to adopt the law. In 2011 it passed a law that municipalities had to separate waste at the source. And since 2017, municipalities can only get incentive grants if they contract with recyclers. This is what unlocked a truly sustainable income for Edilberto's association. Change happened faster as the recyclers themselves, now professionally organized, followed up on the local implementation of laws in hundreds of municipalities. Recyclers became a group that was influential enough to bring industry leaders to the table to negotiate better rates for recycling materials that are sold to other countries.

Following the success in Peru, recyclers gained similar legal protections in Brazil and Ecuador. In 2019, Albina Ruiz became the deputy minister of the environment, where she continued to work on her mission for a clean Peru.

An Audacious Vision, Running on Values (and Principles)

I wanted to find out from Albina, at which point she developed her audacious vision for change. When did she decide to not just make El Agustino cleaner but also tackle the plight of the waste-pickers all over Peru? She told me that all she wanted to do, at the outset, was solve a very immediate problem. To help a city manager, who contracted her as a student, improve his municipal waste management. She didn't start with a grand vision. She was an engineering student, after all. But she wasn't content with just putting Band-Aids over problems. Instead, she kept digging deeper to find out intuitively why these problems persist.

Albina saw the stigmatization of the poor, the corruption, the poor management, and the perverse incentives that drove recyclers like Edilberto to dump waste all over the city. Taken together, these problems required a transformation that went beyond the mechanics of waste management. It required the holistic change of a system, in which the victims would become the protagonists in an effort to clean up Peru. To Albina, it was simple logic. What emerged was a truly transformative vision for change.

Albina never set out to put the Slow Lane Principles into practice. She'd never heard of them. In her upbringing, she was simply taught to always do right by others. She learned the principles by doing. Immersing herself in the problem and listening to understand not just the technical flaws but the underlying human dynamics. She felt deep empathy for the tragic circumstances of families and children like Edilberto. And she was uncompromising when it came to her environmentalist mission.

Trying to get the national law passed a second time proved a turning point for Albina. She stepped aside as the leader to share the agency and let recyclers lead. She chose that path not just because it created a better political dynamic, but because she could not see Ciudad Saludable oversee the implementation of the law in eighteen hundred municipalities. After decades of empowering waste-pickers to improve their livelihoods, it was a logical next step to let them take charge of political negotiations and oversight as well.

Solving For, Solving With

As I approached the Prince George Hotel, it was stunning. Absolutely stunning. Tucked away to the side of Times Square in Manhattan, the grand building was full of stories and mysteries. Walking in, I noticed the kind of all-glass security gates I had seen in fancy office buildings. But as I lingered and observed the coming and going of people, I noticed that this was no fancy office, hotel, or apartment building. The Prince George Hotel offers supported living to formerly homeless or low-income individuals. Half of the tenants live with HIV/AIDS, a mental illness, and/or a history of substance abuse.

Built with Beauty for 416

I first visited in 2012, to meet Rosanne Haggerty. She was one of the driving forces behind the Prince George and bought it in 1995 with Common Ground, a nonprofit she cofounded in 1990. The loving restoration was no indulgence. Design is one of Rosanne's many secret weapons. She believes places shape people and vice versa. As if to underline this point, her own office was simple and austere. It reflects a sense of mission and personal responsibility to do something about poverty and loneliness that had defined her life.

It was a seven-year-long, $48 million journey to turn around a former hotel that had declined into an overcrowded and dysfunctional homeless shelter, housing seventeen hundred people in the 1980s. Raising the necessary funding had been a gigantic lift for Rosanne and her team. New York City provided half the funding through long-term low-interest loans, the other half came from the sale of historic preservation tax credits—a model that allows for the actual sale of tax advantages—and corporate bridge-financing by banks. When the Prince George reopened in 2002, it was the overwhelming beauty and detail that surprised visitors most. It is part of a plan to give dignity to people who are commonly stigmatized. And it provides income: the beautifully restored Prince George Ballroom is also a premium venue for events.

But to succeed, the Prince George needed to be more than just beautiful. Rosanne teamed up with organizations to provide the whole package of services and activities to help people reenter society: case management, training, crafts and art spaces, health care, job support, and social care services. Each partner brought unique capabilities but also funding models that helped sustain the entire operation. The idea behind the Prince George is as simple as it is effective. Give people a stable, safe, and supportive home, and they can focus on important things like finding a job. Community outreach programs even involved neighbors to help the 416 residents of the Prince George Hotel succeed in life.

After the success of the Prince George, Rosanne and Common Ground went on to convert or build more than thirty-two hundred supported affordable housing units, like those provided by the Prince George Hotel, in the states of New York and neighboring Connecticut. And that was just the start.

Built with Truth for 100,000

In 2011, following her work with Common Ground, Rosanne launched a new organization, Community Solutions. Initially the goal was to build one hundred thousand homes in the United States (which they did). Despite its success, however, none of the participating cities ended homelessness. Rosanne and her team identified four underlying issues holding back progress. First, no one was responsible for ending homelessness. Second, people who fund progress only measure the success of their specific investment, not the overall impact on reducing homelessness. Third, data was poor. It was collected only once a year, wasn't accurate, and left out key information. And fourth, the housing system was broken, as newly built stock didn't reduce homelessness.

Rosanne and her team looked for ways to not just serve homeless people, but try to reduce, or even end, homelessness. In 2015 they launched a new, ambitious campaign called "Built for Zero" to end homelessness in American cities. They found that cities had a margin of error of around 240 percent when counting the homeless. A mayor might think they have two thousand homeless people, but the number could be as high as sixty-eight hundred or as low as seven hundred. Why was it so hard to get the right number? Because cities only count the homeless once a year, sending teams out on a single twenty-four-hour mission to find them. The result is not just an unreliable number but also a number that doesn't tell city officials what to do, or what these people need. A generic measure leads officials to offer generic help, not responding to the actual needs of people.

This resonated with Rosanne's first experience working in a homeless shelter in 1982. The shelter offered beds, when what people actually required was help with finding a job and finding a home. What cities need to tackle homelessness is what Rosanne calls "real-time, by name" data on every homeless person. Once you have that, you can solve the problem.

Ending It for 550,000

If data is the problem, how do Rosanne and her team solve it? To get this "real-time, by name" data, Community Solutions brings together all the organizations in a city that come into contact with homeless persons. The police, libraries, shelters, emergency services, nonprofits, faith organizations. People experiencing homelessness are not just interacting with housing experts, they rely on many services. For example, a case of domestic violence may lead to a family breakup that in turn leads to some family members ending up homeless. Social and police services are involved with the people at risk of homelessness, but it is often not their job to consider housing. With the help of Community Solutions these organizations now maintain an up-to-date list of everyone who is experiencing homelessness, always asking their permission to collect personal details. With this new approach city leaders don't just get a generic number, but what specific situation the person is in. As a team, they can determine the specific support needed to get this person out of homelessness.

Does it work? By 2022, 105 cities in the United States had joined Built for Zero. Of these, sixty-four achieved quality real-time data. Forty-two cities reduced homelessness. Fourteen communities—like Abilene, Texas, and Lancaster City, Pennsylvania—achieved what Community Solutions calls "functional zero," which means that they have ended chronic homelessness (people experiencing homelessness for more than a year). Together, they have housed 147,000 people.[4] In 2020, Community Solutions won a $100 million grant from the MacArthur Foundation, to help another seventy-five communities reach functional zero by 2026.

Built Not For, but with 58,000

In 2008, Rosanne wondered if what had worked for the 416 residents of the Prince George Hotel could be applied to Brownsville, a neighborhood of fifty-eight thousand people in Brooklyn. At the time, Brownsville had the highest infant mortality rate in New York City, the highest high school dropout rate, the highest murder rate, and was among the poorest neighborhoods in the city. It was an urban planner's nightmare. Too much public housing left room for little else. The New York City government seemed to have overlooked the neighborhood for decades and was slow to act.

Rosanne's vision was for Brownsville to become a stable neighborhood, safe and supportive for people to build better lives. Like the Prince George, the neighborhood would have to include not just better housing the better public services. But where to start in a neighborhood with so many problems, so much violence, so much neglect? Brownsville is different from the Prince George in important ways. Unlike a building with tenants, it is a neighborhood, with no contracts or gates. And working with 58,000 people going about their daily lives is a different ballgame than working with 416 people who live in supported housing. And unlike the Prince George, the hundreds of services the community receives—from schools to health, welfare to street cleaning, housing to policing—come from different New York City agencies. In Rosanne's mind the way to get involved with Brownsville was to involve its people, to put them in charge.

Seeding Empowerment

Community Solutions got the ball rolling by founding the Brownsville Partnership. They hired residents with deep community connections to become community organizers and had them trained by world-class experts at Harvard University. It was important to hire locally, to develop the skills and the muscle for the Brownsville Partnership to be led and run by the people of Brownsville. Community organizing is much more than a series of meetings. It is a process of listening, building trust, learning, ideation, and holding partners accountable. Done well, the process would allow the residents of Brownsville to become knowledgeable and empowered to shape their destiny and hold New York City agencies accountable.

A critical milestone for the community was to have a plan for their future. In 2017, nine years after the process started, they published the Brownsville Plan and submitted it to the city.[5] Brownsville had a long history of trying to use community organizing to gain more control over public services—most notably, the dramatic events of 1966–69 when local families tried, and ultimately failed, to gain more control over local schooling.[6] In the 1970s outside city planners inflicted further harm on the neighborhood, when they designed great schemes *for* Brownsville instead of *with* Brownsville.

Community organizing was new to Rosanne's work. It took a long time—years in fact—but she saw it as a critical foundation to build on.

Reimagining Early Childhood

The Brownsville Plan was about reimagining Brownsville. One of the priorities, highlighted by families, was to change what it was like to grow up in Brownsville, especially the early childhood experience. People wanted a healthier, more supportive, and safer environment for children and their families. Local people and service providers came together with experts to create United for Brownsville in 2018. Funded by Robin Hood, a nonprofit that fights poverty, United for Brownsville is a partnership between Rosanne's organization, Community Solutions, and SCO, a large nonprofit that provides family services. Their goal is to improve early childhood development, especially the social-emotional learning and language skills of zero to three-year-olds. Their goal: to set children up for equal opportunities in education and life.

In 2021, I spoke with Kassa Belay and David Harrington, the codirectors of what is called the backbone of United for Brownsville. The backbone team facilitates the collaborations among families and service providers. United for Brownsville is unusual in that it is led by both parents and service providers. Twenty-one local family members constitute the Family Advisory Board. The families' lived experiences make them experts, and United for Brownsville pays them for their expertise, as they would pay other expert consultants. More than forty providers of social, education, and health services for infants and toddlers constitute the Provider Action Team. United for Brownsville chose this setup to address the racial inequities and imbalance of power that had defined city services for generations.

Early Intervention is one such service. It is a free service offered by New York City to children zero to three years old who have developmental delays. Parents of Black and Hispanic children in Brownsville were using this service at much lower rates (-30 percent) than in other parts of New York City. The Family Advisory Board investigated this discrepancy by reaching back into their communities. Families reported experiencing several barriers in using Early Intervention. They were afraid of the evaluation process, in which an expert usually visits the home of a child to diagnose them for developmental delays. Families were afraid of these visits, found them intrusive, and felt like their home life would be inspected.

To overcome this fear, United for Brownsville came up with a new approach. Families created a new role at United for Brownsville, the Early Intervention Ambassador, who would help families navigate the Early Intervention system and provide neutral space for meetings. The Family Advisory Board led a recruitment, hiring Danny Herring, an experienced special needs educator from Brooklyn and herself the mother of a child with disabilities.

Everyone Works the Data

Kassa and David point out how important quality data is to the work of United for Brownsville. More than a decade ago, people like Rosanne sensed that New York City public services performed poorly in Brownsville. For years, city agencies dragged their feet to share information with United for Brownsville. But Early Intervention was willing to share data. It showed inequities and led to specific conversations about people, their needs, and what needed to be done to support them. By relying on families as intermediaries, United for Brownsville could reach out to other families in the neighborhood.

In a place where people don't trust officials, this proved critical, just as it had for User Voice in a London prison. Ten years of cultivating trust and developing capabilities in Brownsville were beginning to pay off exponentially when it came to working with this data. Families put the referral data to good use: by 2021 referrals of Black and Hispanic children were practically on par with the rest of the city, with uptake now higher than in any other New York City borough.[7]

Betting on Brownsville started out as a hypothesis, an experiment to let a community take charge. For Rosanne it was quite different from the Prince George and Built for Zero programs, in which her organization had provided the vision and led the charge. In Brownsville it is now families who determine what success will look like. Community Solutions provided patient capital and support to let things start slow, nurturing trust, confidence, and capabilities. Things are falling into place for families working with United for Brownsville. They have gained experiences, and new capabilities, by implementing smaller projects for the first three years. Today, empowered by meaningful data, they appear to have the foot firmly on the accelerator.

From Deep to Wide, to Deep-Wide

Rosanne's mission began by witnessing the ineffectiveness of a homeless shelter in New York City. Over the course of forty years, she was of service with a relentless focus on progress. Her story reveals three big transitions, in which she went from working deep by building housing units to going wide by running national campaigns to end homelessness. In Brownsville her organization helped bring the insights from going deep and wide together. First, it had to slow down, years went by until the community had found its footing. Then things picked up, as families put their capabilities and power to use.

In Rosanne's mind, what connects all pieces of the journey is a passion for putting data to use. Not in a technological sense but as an organizing principle. Unless cities know their homeless people, they cannot end homelessness. And with data, families of Brownsville, officials and professionals can find creative ways that work to transform the neighborhood. Always at the speed of trust.

Social Imagination Is the Love We Give

This chapter has shown how sharing the agency allows people who are often regarded as weak and powerless to take charge and create new answers. I call this collective endeavor social imagination. It is not a dream or ideology but a journey rooted in community and practice. Whether at home, in society, in business, or in government, practicing social imagination brings real joy as we empower people and jointly experiment with new ways of doing.

What Does Good Look Like?

In all three stories in this chapter solutions were not imposed by a singular leader or ideology but emerged out of listening, experimentation, and participation. In Albina's case it was her environmentalism and technical skills that brought her into government. In doing the technical work, she found that her humanity pulled her toward the injustices against waste-pickers as the unbearable cost of a broken system. And the more Albina worked with waste-pickers, she found that they weren't a problem. As recyclers, they could in fact become one of the most valuable resources in fixing the broken waste system.

Reframing: Finding the Radically Better Question

This kind of reframing can be a truly radical first step. Reframing can be practiced with empathy and razor-sharp logic. Albina brought the worlds of waste management, engineering, social justice, and economic empowerment together to create an offering that inspired Edilberto, despite his vulnerability, to take a leap of faith. That is reframing a situation right there, to what matters most! And this unlocks the creative opportunities to imagine what is next. Social imagination begins right there, as we begin to chart a course that is not defined by what anyone had believed to be possible. Instead, it is defined by what is right.

Reframing is at its most powerful when we change the narrative about the people who suffer the consequences of a broken system. Traditionally, they are labeled the disabled, the incompetent, or the victims. Yet in Albina's story there is little talk about "helping victims." Her movement chose to ask: What if those who suffer the most become part of or even own the solution? It is a question that looks for capabilities rather than weaknesses, right from the start.

This is no easy feat. In *Thinking, Fast and Slow*, professor of psychology Daniel Kahneman explains how our lazy brains try to avoid the effort of finding new answers. Instead, our brains pick an answer that is already known to us. Even if it is an answer to an entirely different question. That is what he means by "thinking fast." For Albina, thinking fast would have led her to an engineering solution to waste management. After all, engineering is what she knew, it aligned with her skills, it is what everyone expected (and paid her) to do. And it would have yielded some quick results. According to Kahneman, it is what everybody's brains wanted! But she chose to engage waste-pickers and go out of her way to think slow, not in a technical or authoritarian manner, to find the *right* answer. Slow Lane stories often start by thinking slow, avoiding the temptation of just making the issue go away, instead creating a new frame of reference.

Putting this into practice requires a most uncomfortable first step: letting go of our hard-earned experiences, expectations, knowledge, and know-how. Without a passionate desire to solve a problem or make a difference, people will simply not be motivated to go down this path. To unleash this kind of passion, Slow Lane movements have developed a couple of valuable techniques:

Organizing = Empowering

Organizing, as practiced in the Slow Lane, means empowerment. Typically it starts out as a service. Albina didn't simply drag recyclers to a national negotiating table; she spent *thirty years* supporting, training, and organizing recyclers so that they could join the table from a place of pride and capability. Without this nurturing effort, their precarious lives would have not allowed them to pay attention to anything but their immediate survival. They joined the negotiations not indoctrinated but liberated to be experts at their own lives and their possible futures. We see the same method in the work of Dorica, whose first step was to create a national association, at the service of rare disease patients. And Community Solutions started by funding years of community organizing in Brownsville.

Imagination by Doing

The second technique is simple: trial and error. In all three stories in this chapter we see a lot of experimentation to overcome prejudice and win support and trust from others. It is an unfair truth that movements often have to prove that people who were stigmatized for being poor, uneducated, or uninformed can indeed create, deliver, and own better solutions.

Dorica's NoRo center is a prototype to show how rare disease patients could work alongside families as well as social service and health-care professionals. Albina's movement proved that waste-pickers could team up, to become recycling businesses that were better at managing municipal waste than the so-called professionals with their expensive machines and

corrupt business practices. And United for Brownsville showed
that families could put data and design-thinking methodologies
to good use and help improve early childhood services.

This kind of experimentation is a powerful capability for almost all aspects of Slow Lane movements: like finding out how
to make decisions, how to fund efforts, what political tactics
to use, or how to actually achieve results. Trial and error de-
mocratizes the Slow Lane, making it a place where anyone can
acquire sophisticated skills to imagine real change.

Systemic Change = Empowerment × Practice

To see how radically different all this is, think about Facebook
or Tesla for a moment. Neither company set out to design solutions for those who are disadvantaged or excluded. It would
only have weakened their plans for technological dominance.
For their stories to work, they have to first solve for the most
privileged—the wealthy early adopters, who like to use new
toys and will make them desirable to others. By the time their
products reach people further down the social hierarchy, these
products either impose their terms on people by exploiting the
user's personal data (Facebook) or simply remaining an unaf-
fordable dream (Tesla).

The story of Albina's movement is radically different, however. It is because waste-pickers take charge that it gets more
and more ambitious and transformative over time. The vision
of Slow Lane thinkers feeds on a radical shift of power that
builds a stronger, more inclusive society at every step of the
way. Courageous imagination, here, is not a utopia but the logical product of empowerment and experimentation.

= 4 =

Nurture Curiosity

We tend to formulate our problems in such a way as to make it seem that the solutions to those problems demand precisely what we already happen to have at hand.

Abraham Kaplan

If all you have is a hammer,
everything looks like a nail.

Abraham Maslov

Abraham Kaplan and Abraham Maslov were concerned that scientists, charged with the pursuit of truth, tailor their questions to fit their abilities to answer them. The Fast Lane goes a step further still: in its pursuit for dominance, it wants its quick fixes to become the solution for all problems. So when it comes to the hammer and the nail, the Fast Lane would say, "My hammer is the answer to everything!"

The Fast Lane way of solving problems and creating change is to lock into one answer and stick to it. A brilliant leader, in this logic, is one who knew the right answer from the start. And once the Fast Lane gets invested in a solution, it has to insist that nothing else can work. Since people find change tedious, it only feels natural to operate in this way. That's especially true if you need to show a return on your investment by growing your market share or by taking credit for your actions. The Fast Lane ends up using all powers at its disposal to prove it is right. And since people with considerable power are in charge, they have a lot of means at their disposal to do just that. Business leaders, for example, can buy up competitors to stay on top or lobby governments to get favorable regulations to secure their dominance. Soon it no longer matters whether these answers are right, or that they only help a small group of people. A successful Fast Lane leader can bend the world to fit their answer.

The Slow Lane does things differently. In the Slow Lane, movements succeed by nurturing their curiosity, in a constant quest to find better answers. They keep their options open. Built for Zero doesn't prescribe any one way for community leaders to solve homelessness. Instead, it encourages local leaders to find out what works best for them. What Built for Zero does insist on is that leaders get better at counting and understanding the people who experience homelessness. This kind of flexibility makes it much easier for local leaders to buy into Built for Zero and become cocreators of the solutions. They feel empowered, not imposed on. It helps Built for Zero respond to changing circumstances and individual needs and to stay open to new ideas and insights.

To nurture curiosity, the Slow Lane encourages learning and experimentation. It seeks inspiration from outside, learning from science, arts, or other movements. Not locked into just one answer, Slow Lane movements remain open and inviting to others. Think about it: Would you rather join a group that demands that you submit to their ideology, or one that invites you to come as your full self and make a contribution? The German Green Party institutionalized this. The path to the top is always open, for any member. And the rare disease movement in Romania invites doctors, nurses, journalists, and government ministries into the movement. They don't have to opt into a fixed solution but can play their part in empowering patients.

This chapter on nurturing curiosity follows three stories that are dear and personal to me. As a social entrepreneur, I have suffered through countless setbacks and the full set of emotions that these entail. In the first story, "Meet the Zombies," we start with just such an experience, by returning to Mark Johnson and User Voice. We dive into the pain of rejection they experienced, to shine a light on a choice: Should we feed on our prejudice and frustration to pin blame on the government, or could we approach a setback with curiosity to uncover something deeper? Opting for curiosity, we discover the zombies, big bureaucratic systems that have lost all direction. In further pursuit of zombies, the second story, "Fifty Years Late for Everything," follows the evidence of why Chicago's street crossings are so unwelcoming to people with visual impairments. It leads us to a zombie system that could have prevented this from happening: city procurement. And in the last story, "Flipping a Zombie? Delightful Bureaucracy," we follow my journey to turn city government procurement into a force for real change, by using some unconventional sources of inspiration along the way.

Curiosity works in four ways: First, if we can unlearn our preconceptions, curiosity can help us see past frustration and prejudice to reveal the zombies, the real underlying problems. This kind of unlearning lets us change our perspective. Second, we can use this openness to build new bridges that activate people in power, to become our new allies. Third, curiosity owns what is broken, meaning that we take responsibility even for problems that aren't ours. Nurturing curiosity lets us look beyond traditional answers, tap into new forms of inspiration, and give outsiders permission to get involved. Fourth, curiosity lets us walk in on our bureaucracies or other systems to change things. As we arrive at these unexpected places, we should feel proud of being imposters, helping to reimagine and fix what is broken.

What is so special about the Slow Lane is that by sharing the agency it creates the space for everyone to contribute to a new emerging vision for change. Curiosity, practiced in this way, helps us retain the flexibility to find common ground, instead of getting caught up on a single solution.

Meet the Zombies

London, summer of 2020. Scheduling a meeting with Mark Johnson was hard. He canceled twice because his sheep kept jumping the fences of his farm. At last, we had a chance to talk about how close he came to changing the UK's criminal justice system. Before we get there, let me remind you of just how unlikely it was for Mark to become the owner of a farm, never mind a powerful influencer of national criminal justice policy. As a child, he survived severe domestic violence, slipping into crime and substance abuse as a teenager. Child protection and support systems didn't work for Mark, and as a young adult, he went in and out of prison. Eventually his addiction led him to become a homeless person in central London with a $600-a-day heroin habit.

Again and again, Mark slipped out of programs meant to return him to sobriety and to society. When at last he overcame his addiction, he discovered his entrepreneurial talent. Success in running his landscaping business brought stability. With stability, he was able to come to terms with his trauma. By the time he was thirty-five years old in 2005, Charles, the then Prince of Wales, retold Mark's story at the Young Achiever of the Year Award ceremony.

The Very Unlikely Expert

Mark knew better than anyone that his success was the lucky escape from a dangerous trajectory that could have ended his life early. His life story is a reminder of how children who suffer abuse can get caught up in crime, and how hard it is to help someone trapped in addiction, a dysfunctional family, poverty, and homelessness. Mark learned that he succeeded whenever his desire to move on coincided with exactly the right support.

In 2009, Mark started User Voice, a nonprofit to improve the criminal justice system. His idea was that when we give ex-offenders a voice in their rehabilitation journey, they are more likely to succeed. Mark hoped to help people like his former self succeed and break their cycle of returning to crime. The government stood to benefit too if this led to a lower rate of recidivism, the rate of crimes committed by ex-offenders. It worked. Independent evaluations of User Voice in prisons and communities across the country had proven that if you listen to ex-offenders in the right way, you can better respond to their needs along their rehabilitation journey. As a result, prisons were safer, and more people succeeded at rebuilding their lives.

Calling out the Quick-Fix Nonsense

In 2013, Chris Grayling, the UK Secretary of State for Justice, announced "Transforming Rehabilitation," a major redesign of the probation and rehabilitation system. The goal was to lower the persistently high rate of recidivism. By this time, Mark had become a renowned and sought-after expert, and a widely published advocate to improve rehabilitation outcomes.

With evidence to back his approach, User Voice and its supporters saw an opportunity to help. Without strings attached, Mark offered the government to help build their own version of User Voice, as an independent government function. They demonstrated how using high-quality feedback to better target support services could save half a billion pounds ($670 million) a year. If the government didn't take up his proposal, Mark feared, the reform effort would remain detached from the actual needs of the ex-offenders. Without the right support they would end up reoffending.

The government rejected Mark's proposal without serious consideration, citing a minor budgetary pretext. His worst fears came true, as he watched the disastrous reform unfold. The National Audit Office (NAO) concluded in 2019 that with Transforming Rehabilitation "the government had set itself up for failure from the start."[1] It called the reform overly simplistic, relying on too little data, and paying no attention to the people using the system. In true Fast Lane fashion, the NAO found, reform measures were rushed to save money quickly, without prior testing or consultation. By 2017 reoffenses had shot up by 22 percent. In 2019 the costly reform was rolled back in its entirety. Over its course, it had derailed the rehabilitation of hundreds of thousands of ex-offenders.

At a time of severe budget austerity, the reform effort wasted billions, money that was taken from the kind of community services that prevent crime in the first place. To the government, Mark had never been more than a blip on the bureaucratic radar. To Mark, it was a devastating blow because he knew the struggles of the many people trapped in the probation system. And he was left feeling powerless and unseen by the government he tried to help. Society ended up paying dearly, becoming less safe as a result: following the reform, the crime rate went up by 140 percent.[2]

Taking It Like a Person Who Cares

Even seven years after this setback, I still hear deep hurt in Mark's voice as he recounts the experience. He suspects that he was brushed off because his approach, and his life story, were incompatible with a criminal justice bureaucracy that defined itself by a "tough on crime agenda." Mark tells me that one reason he turned to permaculture farming was to overcome this disillusionment. He wants to regain his strength and hope by building a new, better community, quite literally from the ground up.

Social change theories or textbooks are strong on success stories but rarely mention the frequent pain and even trauma of setbacks experienced by people like Mark. Naturally, no one likes setbacks or seeing an opportunity go to waste. But the bumps in the Slow Lane can be psychologically more devastating because they involve so many people at the periphery of our systems who have lived experience of the problem they are trying to solve.

Changing things also requires that institutions play along. Many have professionalized, signaling that they will do what works to achieve the best outcomes. What that means in practice is that they need solutions that are viable, with evidence to prove their effectiveness in both cost and outcomes. User Voice had readied itself for years to offer a compelling proposition: a solution that is proven to work, that is guaranteed to save costs, supported by a wide community and not asking for much in return. Anticipating a thorough vetting, User Voice had meticulously carried out independent evaluations and built their reputation in the field.

What happened next came as a surprise. According to Mark, the very government department in charge of rehabilitating ex-offenders couldn't look past its prejudice against ideas from ex-offenders like him. Intentional or not, when no real evaluation or formal hearing took place, Mark took it as a clear signal: we don't want to hear you.

The Bumps Should Give Us Pause

User Voice is not alone in experiencing this pain. Thousands of Slow Lane movements experience similar setbacks. And setbacks can be a natural, healthy part of the process: nudging us to go back to the drawing board, refine ideas, share more power, collect evidence, or build more bridges. But as Mark's story shows, they can also be arbitrary, contradicting the stated purpose of our institutions. As I met with Slow Lane movements around the world, almost all of them told me about being brushed off by governments without a fair evaluation. These stories came in from movements dealing with very different governments and circumstances: from Barcelona to Buenos Aires, London to Lagos, the Navajo Nation to New York, and Singapore to Sweden. I feel their pain because I experienced many setbacks myself. And it is especially people like Mark, who step up from the unlikeliest biographies to change things for the better, whom governments should be paying attention to.

As you read this, you may shake your head at the usual suspects: governments, politicians, bureaucrats. But I urge you to also remember the creative and empathetic work by public servants in Sefton; or how Kevin Reilly, the governor of Pentonville Prison, worked with User Voice to break with 172 years to work with prisoners. In my twenty years of working with government officials all over the world, I never really met a cynical public servant. Whenever I followed up to hear the government's side of the story, I found people who cared and who wanted to improve things. (That said, I was unable to get a meaningful reaction from the UK Prison & Probation System about their handling of User Voice.) Plenty of people in government would like to bring about positive change, and I have found plenty of examples where Slow Lane movements included government leaders.

Don't Blame People, Blame the Zombies

If we can't pin blame on officials, then who is to blame for these setbacks? I have followed the trail to find out what is going on. What I found is that some institutions end up producing entirely unwanted and arbitrary outcomes. They have turned into bureaucracies that lack a mission and purpose to guide their actions. Whatever they do, becomes their purpose, not the other way around. I call these the zombie systems, and by understanding them, we can begin to change them.

Fifty Years Late for Everything

Here is what it takes to cross a street without eyesight. Find the crossing; align yourself correctly; fix your bearings; memorize what the traffic signal does; trust that no straggling vehicles are making a run; calculate how much time you will have to make the crossing; hope for the best. Walk. To change that, Marburg, a small city in Germany, started to install audible traffic signals in 1971. Sounds provide cues to help blind and low-vision people make a crossing. In 2021, a full fifty years after Marburg had begun its upgrade, Chicago, Illinois, had equipped just 11 of its 2,672 traffic signals with such audible aids.

By 2021, Marburg had become the self-proclaimed Blinden-stadt Marburg (Marburg, city for the blind). Many experts consider it the most blind-friendly city in the world. Once all traffic signals were audible, the city began to systematically break down other barriers. Visually impaired people found ever more access as well as experiences of joy and new opportunities for personal growth. In Marburg bus stops are audible; special pavement textures help navigation; walking tours and tactile models of historical sights help exploration; buildings offer tactile floor plans in their entrance areas; and planners designed their award-winning renovation of the central station around the needs of the visually impaired. Local leaders continue to push new boundaries, aiming to grow the number of blind and low-vision students in natural science courses at the university, even breaking down barriers to lab sciences like chemistry. It is not surprising, then, that a third of all blind students in Germany choose to study at the University of Marburg.

You can easily imagine how different the experience of those fifty years would have been to visually impaired people in Marburg and Chicago. Differences in personal freedoms or in the level of stress in completing daily routines. How these cities dealt with traffic signals had a direct impact on the life prospects and opportunities of thousands of people. Why, then, did Chicago fall fifty years behind Marburg? Those fifty years held back not just the prospects of thirty-six thousand visually impaired Chicagoans but also weighed heavily on family members, volunteers, and government services, who all had to step up to fill the gaps. How did Chicago miss almost three thousand opportunities to install better traffic signals?

What happened? It wasn't a lack of money. Chicago is wealthier than Marburg, where GDP per person is $38,000, compared with $61,000 in Chicago. From a budget perspective, the City of Chicago spends $11 billion a year—about the same per resident as the City of Marburg—and the cost of upgrading 2,672 signalized traffic intersections would amount to just $15 million. That's 0.1 percent of the city budget in a year, or $5 per Chicagoan. Invented in the 1920s, the technology has been widely known to traffic engineers since the 1960s. Over the course of these fifty years, the upgrade would have cost just ten cents per resident per year. And it would have been easy to do, since all of Chicago's traffic signals were installed, or replaced, during this period.

A Trip down the Rabbit Hole

When I began to investigate what happened, I made a simple assumption. Governments of major cities know how to make good plans, and they have a lot of technical capacity. Chicago, for instance, employs thirty-five thousand people, of which four thousand work in the departments of streets, sanitation, and transportation. That's a lot of design, engineering, and project management capacity. And the leadership was supportive. In 2003, Mayor Daley of Chicago called for more rights for people with disabilities and for more people with disabilities to be hired into the city government.[3] I doubt that anyone at city hall was opposed to helping visually impaired people thrive. Something must have stopped them from doing what was so evidently right.

Interviews with officials got me nowhere, so I collected more stories. I wanted to find out what happens in other areas of public service, and how this played out in other cities. A surprising new pattern emerged: this shocking fifty-year delay happened wherever I looked—in education, transport, social care, workforce development, energy, construction, public safety, technology. What appeared to be a scandalous exception for the visually impaired in Chicago was actually the norm around the world. It seems to take fifty years to adopt what was proven to work elsewhere. Putting my detective cap on, I took note of my new assumptions:

1. Governments mostly have the right intentions.

2. They have (a lot of) money and capacity.

3. They have good people.

4. But many public services are fifty years behind what works.

5. I could not find a single government anywhere in the world that did *not* have this problem.

6. Nothing seems to stop cities from *not* doing the right thing.

Who Checks for What Works?

That last point (6) on the list really puzzled me. How could we run all these governments with no safeguard against *not* upgrading to what works? Talking to officials, I learned mostly about rules and regulations intended to stop these bureaucracies from doing something wrong. But nothing seemed to demand what is *right*. It took a lawsuit by visually impaired people and the US Department of Justice to force change in 2019, leading to a commitment by Mayor Lightfoot to begin upgrading traffic signals.[4] Chicago wasn't alone. None of the cities I studied had controls in place to make sure they do the *right* thing.

"Follow the money." That's what people say in detective stories. So I, too, followed the money because all governments spend money on traffic signals and everything else. When a government spends public money, it uses a highly regulated process called public procurement. I was hoping to find some answers by looking at how that actually works. Now please, stay with me, this is where we get to the zombies!

How They Spend $6 Trillion

Every government relies on external providers to deliver its services. They buy meals, schoolbooks, security services, cleaning services, cars and trucks, software, construction works, planning and engineering services, childcare, social care, probation services, and traffic signals. Taken together, the world's cities and towns alone spend over $6 trillion a year to procure such goods and services.[5] That's almost a tenth of all money going around in our economy. Without public procurement, we would have no public service. Governments have created a universal set of principles to select who wins business with the city: the process has to be open to competition, meaning that any business or organization should be able to present a proposal for a contract opportunity. It has to be fair, meaning that you cannot discriminate against anyone who presents a good proposal. And it has to be transparent, meaning that all information is available to everyone, with a clear process to guide decisions. This is how government spending works everywhere.

The Misunderstanding That Revealed the Zombie

I stumbled into the zombie hidden in public procurement by way of a simple misunderstanding. In my mind, the principles of competition, fairness, and transparency meant that procurement is trying to not just get the lowest price but also the best idea. Or, explained in the language of traffic signals: a city should automatically learn about the benefits of audible signals whenever they run a competition to buy traffic signals. The reason I believed that things work this way was my background in architecture. In architecture, governments don't simply buy buildings; they run design competitions to find the best solution for their needs.

Architecture competitions use the procurement principles to quite wonderful effect. Teams present different designs responding to a brief. You can see the results of such competitions all over the world. Sydney's iconic Opera House was procured through a design competition in 1957. Two hundred architects from around the world presented their ideas. A jury selected the iconic design of a young Danish architect, Jørn Utzon, to be the winner. It was a complex decision, weighing the risks of building a technically complicated project against the public benefit of gaining a landmark, acoustic qualities, and costs involved. The ideas presented at the time were all radically different, each representing a different way forward. In my amateur's mind, if this was how cities spend their money, it provided a good way to evaluate different ideas before deciding what traffic signals to buy or how to deliver a public service.

Soon enough, people taught me about how public procurement actually worked. In reality, cities did not use the way they spend their money to improve services. Instead, procurement was a bureaucracy with the purpose of protecting the bureaucracy. Here is what that means: whenever a government spends money, it is afraid of breaking a law or causing a scandal. If you have heard about public procurement, it is usually because of a scandal. In Germany, for example, where I live, everyone has heard about the cost overruns of the Hamburg Philharmonic (the project ended up costing twenty times more than planned) or the delays to opening the Berlin airport (a decade late, costing three times more than planned).

Famously, in the United States, everyone remembers the collapse of healthcare.gov, the flagship online marketplace of Obamacare as soon as it launched. Or more recently, the corruption and cronyism involved in buying urgent supplies during the early days of the Covid-19 pandemic. With time, governments have tried to protect themselves against these embarrassing and costly scandals by creating ever tighter rules for procurement. Sadly, these rules focus entirely on avoiding scandal and say nothing about finding ways to better serve the public. As a result, the principles of transparency, fairness, and open competition are mere boxes to be checked—not a source of improvement.

When Buying Frankenstein Outcomes Is the Norm

A bureaucracy that has no other purpose than to protect itself cannot be effective at serving the public. In Chicago the procurement of traffic signals may have succeeded in protecting the bureaucracy. But for visually impaired people, the outcomes were simply terrible. For fifty years, despite the best intentions to support people with disabilities, no one seems to have noticed. It was only when the Department of Justice joined a legal case presented by the visually impaired people of Chicago that things began to change.

What happened to visually impaired folks in Chicago is just a tiny facet of a much bigger problem. Cities provide hundreds of public services, of which making street crossings work for everyone is only one. Public procurement touches almost everything important we experience in our lives. It is less a matter of how much governments spend than *how* they spend that determines our quality of life. Procurement can make your air cleaner, enable you to learn better at school, give you safer streets, provide cleaner water, and put more services within your reach. It can give you a fair chance in life.

All this brokenness in procurement is the norm. Procurement causes the same pain in Marburg as it does in Chicago. Marburg achieved remarkable results for visually impaired people, not because it runs a superior government. Instead, it was a kink of history that led for blista, Germany's first educational institute for the blind, to be opened in Marburg a hundred years ago. The school pushed Marburg to become a hotbed of advocacy and innovation for the blind.[6] Daily news reports show that the city lags decades behind in many other areas, such as digitization. During the Covid-19 pandemic, for instance, school children regularly took to the street in protest, demanding better schooling.

First, Spot the Zombie

Earlier I wrote that zombie systems undermine even the best-intentioned public leader. Procurement is one such system. Zombie systems are power structures in government that reliably produce unintended outcomes. They have no real purpose or oversight but wield considerable influence over all kinds of important public goods—like health, safety, mobility, housing, education, air quality, water, social care, opportunity, equality. I refer to them as zombies because they aren't behaving as expected, or in line with a mission. Our governments can want something quite different from what they produce. It is a bit like throwing a game of dice into the process of social change. We can find such zombie systems whenever we look beyond a single story and discover why change isn't happening.

Public procurement ticks all these boxes. People had become so accustomed to how public procurement worked that they stopped asking why. Blinded by big scandals, they overlooked a much bigger problem: governments miss countless opportunities to improve things. Fifty years is a lifetime. And if procurement could have bettered the lives of visually impaired people decades ago, it could have done so with all other needs. It might have turned around the UK's doomed prison and probation reform, by insisting they consider the viable proposal presented by User Voice. But instead of correcting mistakes, procurement kept replicating them for decades.

Then Tame It

I want to end this section on an upbeat note. Zombie systems can be fixed, but how? First, systems like public procurement must be given a meaningful purpose. In the next story I share my experience in following my dream of turning public procurement into a creative force for good. It is a prototype of how we can breathe new meaning into a zombie system.

Flipping a Zombie? Delightful Bureaucracy

As a child, my all-too-vivid imagination had gotten me into plenty of trouble. At one point I convinced all the children in my kindergarten that my family would be traveling to the moon for the winter holidays. Much to the dismay of their parents, who now had to deal with children who complained about their less spectacular vacation plans.

Daydreaming with Tired Bureaucracies

Maybe it was this all-too-vivid imagination that got me to see an opportunity deep inside the bureaucracy of government. Just like I had never been an astronaut, I certainly had no qualifications related to public procurement. But it did seem part of an important problem that I was acutely aware of: everywhere I went, I found that cities took far too long to improve their public services in ways that worked for everyone. Procurement fascinated me because it was everywhere, and yet no one knew about it. I kept wondering, Could we use the bureaucratic process by which city governments spend money, to help our public services stay with the times?

Our dream was audacious. We were a tiny team with a few thousand euros in the bank and no power whatsoever. Municipalities, by comparison, employed millions of people and spent trillions of dollars, or 8 percent of the world's GDP, every year. Municipalities buy the goods and services that shape our lives: public services in health, education, transport, social care, economic opportunity, and energy all rely on procurement. In 2009, when we started to float the idea of turning public procurement into a force for good, unsurprisingly, everyone told us not to waste our energy.

In the words of one of our most senior mentors: "Governments prefer not to talk about it because it is embarrassing that they don't know how to spend the billions entrusted to them well. Business leaders are afraid to speak up for fear of losing trust of their government clients. And the public only ever learn about scandals, not successes." And yet he also agreed that if somehow we could turn public procurement from being a zombie system that puts a break on social change, to becoming a force for better outcomes, it would be a considerable win for everyone. So we tried.

A Beginner's Mind

Here is what I had in mind when we started. I wanted public procurement to work more like the architecture design competitions I was familiar with. Instead of telling suppliers what to do, could governments invite companies, movements, and organizations to submit their ideas on how best to solve the problem? This would be a great way to keep cities open to new ideas. It would also make it harder to keep buying the same ineffective solutions for decades, like Chicago's traffic signals that are of no use to people with low vision.

This idea had grown on me over the six years we had run a global network of living laboratories. In these living labs, we had helped city governments improve their services by involving people, researchers, startups, and corporations. As solutions came out of these labs, so did the question of how to bring them to other cities. But leaders in those other cities showed little interest in our ideas. Many simply ignored or rejected them. Or they said: "I love what you invented in Tallinn—can we invent that in my city also?" It seemed incredibly wasteful to reinvent the wheel in every town and city, frustrating inventors, and spending a lot more time and money than building on what works elsewhere. Stockholm, for example, spent several years and millions of euros on a contract with IBM to develop a mobile payment system for on-street parking. For just 30,000 euros, they could have bought a better solution used by nearby Tallinn, Estonia.

Can a $15,000 Pilot Change a $6 Trillion System?

We spent years trying to overcome this sharing problem. By late 2009, with just 12,000 euros in our accounts, we decided to give procurement a try. We invited cities to publish their needs as a competition, open to new ideas. We hoped that this would provide a more orderly process to find the best way to solve a problem. Nine cities took part in this quick and dirty pilot: Barcelona, Caceres, Chicago, Eindhoven, La Selva, Oeiras, Sant Cugat, Stockholm, and Taipei. Instead of a detailed description of what they wanted to buy, each city posted a clear description of the problem they wanted to solve. Cities promised to pick one winner each and support them to demonstrate their solution as a real-life pilot. Within a couple of months, 317 innovators from around the world presented their ideas. After another six months actual pilots got under way in two of the nine cities. One, Barcelona, tested water sensors to reduce the amount of water needed to irrigate parks and green areas.

Our experiment yielded some promising results. Cities told us that they learned about many new ideas: 308 of the 317 solutions presented were entirely new to them. This made them think harder about whether they could deliver their municipal services differently. Procurement made this learning more formal. Each city had a jury of internal and external experts to evaluate the solutions and select a winner. Despite the fact that we had run this process on a shoestring, for the first time it yielded better outcomes than all other, more elaborate attempts so far. It felt like a real Eureka! moment for us, and we decided to do more of this. We called this process "problem-based procurement" or "procurement challenges."

Do More of What Works

When you want to change things, people keep asking "Why now?" Governments were notoriously sensitive about tinkering with procurement. They were afraid of risks and lacked imagination of what could be possible. What motivated cities to participate was not so much a desire to tackle their procurement bureaucracies. What they really wanted was to connect and be seen together as innovators. They wanted to tell citizens, businesses, and entrepreneurs: "We are a great place for people who have new ideas. Look, even our procurement is open!" Problem-based procurement turned out to be a great way to attract people with ideas.

To move forward, we needed more evidence to prove that problem-based procurement works. We turned our pilot into an annual campaign called "LLGA: Cities Pilot the Future," which gave governments a way to try out this new idea. This format helped us win over mayors who were afraid that acknowledging a problem could be seen as an admission of failure. Our campaign presented participating cities as a global cohort of pioneers, looking for new ways to update their public services. Within just three years we had run more than forty such experiments. City governments kept getting better at solving problems in this way, opening their doors to more ideas from other cities and social innovators. Cape Town, for example, adopted a proven solution for citizen participation from the small city of York in the UK. Cities told us that for the first time public procurement had provided them a jolt of inspiration, showing just how creative they could be.

How "I Trust You" Becomes the New Normal

Every new procurement revealed new insights, often exceeding our expectations. Cities learned about thirty new solutions in each procurement. We discovered that the winning ideas came from surprising places: 98 percent of winners were small businesses, 50 percent were minority- or women-owned businesses. Most of them had been unknown to government buyers. Cities found that these new partners did not just offer better ideas but were also more reliable and committed to good outcomes. Officials found they spent less time managing conflicts with suppliers and more time on improving services.

Cities were becoming less fearful and more outgoing. San Francisco, for example, involved citizens in testing new technologies when the city procured an upgrade of eighteen thousand streetlights to energy-saving LEDs. Citizens appreciated the pilot installations but were concerned about privacy. The city ended up saying no to the kind of smart lighting systems that in 2020 led to civil liberties outcries in San Diego, where the city police used cameras embedded in streetlights to surveil participants in Black Lives Matter protests.[7] Other cities invited citizens, and even children, to join the evaluation committees that selected winning solutions. Social and urban innovators rewarded this openness: 93 percent of participants who did not win contracts reported that they still enjoyed and trusted the process. This reputation for being fair and open paid off, as more than thirty thousand organizations chose to participate in public procurement for the first time.

To keep going with all of this, our team needed a viable business model. We took the simplest path and shared costs and effort among all the participants. Cities paid small participation fees. Companies helped as sponsors and exhibitors at our beautiful events. And every year we had a host city that welcomed program participants and provided the event logistics. As this model began to work, we founded Citymart, to operate and improve the procurement process. With time, we found investors, funders, and partners who shared our dream and helped us stay on mission.

Going Local, Going Deep

By 2013 we noticed that things had changed. Cities talked less about risks and more about wanting to use procurement to tackle some of their chronic social and environmental problems. We took this as a sign that they were more comfortable and willing to tackle more serious issues. At the same time, we noticed that cities had become much better at framing their needs, getting closer to the real social and economic root causes. Their goal was now notably less about connecting with other cities and more about using their bureaucracy to solve problems, and to use procurement to communicate their new priorities.

Barcelona was at the forefront of this development, looking to procurement as a way to connect their exceptional skills for innovation and economic promotion to the deep social inequities in the city. In 2013 the city's unemployment rate had reached 23.7 percent, up from 5.7 percent in 2007. Together with the team of Mayor Xavier Trias, we developed a new program with the goal of redirecting funding from generic startup support programs, to focus on ventures that improve the city. The mayor wanted to signal that everyone could win business with the city and to make problem-based procurement a part of city operations. The result was the Barcelona Open Challenge, a groundbreaking procurement, worth 1 million euros, to solve six urgent needs in the city.[8]

The Barcelona Open Challenge made procurement much simpler and easy to understand for anyone. Legal documents were concise and used simple language. It was the first procurement to have a real public advertising campaign, inviting everyone to participate. Whereas a normal procurement is seen by just twenty people, Barcelona engaged thirty-five thousand citizens in the campaign, and twenty thousand more outside the city. One hundred twenty teams presented proposals, many of them upstarts led by citizens. The challenge succeeded as a procurement, too. The six winning solutions ended up using just 70 percent of the budget. One of them, Vincles, even went on to win the Bloomberg Mayors Challenge, a 5 million euro prize, for tackling the social isolation of thousands of elderly people in the city.[9]

In 2014–15, New York City and Moscow followed Barcelona's lead and embedded the problem-based procurement approach in their bureaucracies. Many others followed. In all, Citymart ran problem-based procurements with 135 cities, on all continents. Three thousand public servants participated, receiving applied training to develop their new skills and mind-sets. Today, professionals around the world use problem-based procurement more and more, supported by a growing ecosystem of hundreds of consultancies and nonprofits who offer support and promote this replication. Their experimentation leads to further improvement and local adaptations. In one case, for example, practitioners in the government of Outer Hebrides, Scotland, were inspired by the Barcelona Open Challenge to put citizens of all ages in charge of procuring their new public transport service.[10]

Has the Zombie Been Flipped?

I am writing about procurement in *The Slow Lane* because it is one of those bureaucratic systems that produces unwanted outcomes in society. It is the cause of frustration and pain. This story illustrates how we may go about putting bureaucracies everywhere to better use. Has all this flipped the zombie system of public procurement? I don't think so. But we may have achieved a mind-set shift, a change in how people think about procurement. Professionals have seen what is possible and are more empowered than ever to make their own journey to change. It will still take decades to change all bureaucracies. Communities are now taking the first steps, and their old zombie systems are starting to look a lot more like Slow Lane movements. As they reimagine what is possible, they breathe new life into procurement.

That's a big shift from 2009, when change seemed impossible. And what we imagined then has now come within reach. If you look carefully, you can even see examples of the Slow Lane Principles practiced in public procurement. (If you are interested in more examples, take a look at my report on the emerging future of city procurement for the Chicago Council on Global Affairs, "Serving the Citizens, Not the Bureaucracy," cited in the chapter notes).

Could this be the beginning of the end for these zombies?

The Four Ways of Nurturing Curiosity

This chapter has explored how the painful bumps in the Slow Lane can be powerful moments to practice curiosity and reveal the zombie systems that undermine all our efforts. And how we may go about flipping those broken systems into forces for real change.

Curiosity Reveals the Zombies

For Mark Johnson and his team, rejection felt deeply personal because it seemed so prejudicial against their biographies, and arbitrary, paying no heed to the impeccable evidence they had assembled to make their case. Mark's story, and our investigation of why Chicago's traffic signals had failed the blind and visually impaired for fifty years, revealed the importance of not rushing to simplistic conclusions as we experience the pain of rejection. It is tempting to pin blame for our setbacks on people in power, like public servants, but doing this we risk deepening the divisions among us. Our impulse to blame people distracts us from investigating what caused these setbacks in the first place. Did the rejection signal a valuable learning moment to refine our ideas? Or was it unintended, produced by a zombie system, something broken buried deep inside our bureaucracies? Even at our most vulnerable, we should try to practice curiosity, to stay open-minded enough to uncover what is broken, even if it is hard to find.

My journey, to tackle public procurement, is just one idea about how we can put curiosity to practice and turn around a zombie system. It is easy for us to overlook bureaucratic systems like public procurement because they appear so far removed from the people we are trying to help. It is easy to expect that it is someone else's job to fix these systems, since we are not in a position of power. And yet they are worth fixing because they have such a big impact on our lives. They exist because people like us never got involved.

Procurement plays a role in almost all the stories told so far in this book. It produces the probation services in the UK, decides who does waste collection in Peru or how Sefton provides supported living services, and determines whether infrastructure ends up serving blind people in Chicago. If we stay alert and creative to spot opportunities, we can set our mind to transform these systems. Collectively we can flip them from being a barrier to becoming an enabler of progress.

Curiosity Builds a Bridge, Even When It Hurts

The Slow Lane is all about perspective. Once the immediate satisfaction has worn off, blaming people does nothing to bring them into the fold. The idea of zombie systems helps us draw an important distinction between broken bureaucracies and the capacity for kindness and good intentions of the people who work in them. Blaming people misses the point. If we can overcome our impulse to blame someone, we can get a double win. We can lay the foundations for our success by building bridges, and we can get started with the interesting task of looking for the real cause of rejection.

This is easier said than done. Slow Lane movements get started because something is broken, and people in power are often part of the problem. Their Fast Lane ways leave many people behind. Successful journeys toward change find ways to activate people in power, by giving them a chance to learn, to develop empathy, to discover a different path. For fifty years Chicago failed to build traffic signals that serve the blind, not because political leaders didn't want them, but *despite* their desire to help the disabled. It is only when we hold this contradiction—seeing terrible outcomes and giving leaders the benefit of the doubt—that we can discover systems that are in urgent need of fixing, that don't work for anyone.

Curiosity Owns What's Broken

The fact that everyone called public procurement a "government bureaucracy" told me something about their expectations. It immediately removed procurement from our lives, signaling a system bound by unchangeable rules, for experts only. Maybe that's how blind people in Chicago felt about their useless traffic signals. Unapproachable, bound by unchangeable rules and regulations. This label isn't inevitable. We don't refer to primary schools, community playgrounds, or care homes as "government bureaucracies." We call them public services. We expect public services to work for us, for everyone. And increasingly we have come to expect to be involved. That's why parents, teachers, and children have elected representation in

schools. Or why Sefton invited people with disabilities to define what "independent living" meant to them. Curiosity helped
challenge that label and led us to call public procurement a
public service. That was liberating and motivated professionals
to open up. And it gives outsiders permission to get involved.

Curiosity Unites Imposters, to Fix It

I used "Delightful Bureaucracy" in the title for the story about
Citymart to challenge our preconceptions, to reframe what
success looks like. We can imagine delightful playgrounds
but struggle to imagine delightful bureaucracies like public
procurement. Both are public services. As we tackle the hidden systems that undermine our common desire for positive
change, we should allow ourselves to dream. Be audacious.

Over the course of ten years, Citymart reimagined public
procurement as a public service through a big collaborative
effort. Thirty thousand businesses and organizations, three
thousand public servants, 135 governments, and dozens of nonprofits, philanthropies, donors, funders, and sponsors came together to change the system, united by a simple idea. We were
just a small group of people facilitating this process, providing
formats and impulses to help the community learn and behave
differently. Overall, no part was worth more than any other,
all relationships mattered. It was only in this context that we
could dare to ask if a $15,000 pilot might be enough to change a
$6 trillion system.

Walking in on our bureaucracies to demand change is the
most helpful thing we can do! We should not be afraid to invite
ourselves to the party. Unless we show up, bureaucracies will
continue to do what they have done for generations: call on se-
cretive management consultants to streamline broken systems.
The problem is, a more efficient broken system is still a broken
system. What these systems really need, more often than not,

is to reimagine their purpose not their workflows. By nurturing curiosity, the Slow Lane is the ideal partner to make this happen.

When it comes to curiosity, feeling like an imposter is a sign that you're doing something right. It brought you to that unexpected place from which you can achieve real change.

= 5 =

Use Technology as an Enabler

Humility, to me, is not about lowering yourself, it's
about how we create space for other voices and draw
the circle bigger with our muscles and our love.

Eric Dawson

Technology holds a glorious promise. It promises unprecedented scale at little cost. At its best, technology unlocks the kind of platform dynamics that become a flywheel, effortlessly leading to ever greater reach and success. Whether this success will help to tackle the "always" problems, and make a meaningful contribution, depends on whether it is used to dominate or to enable people to participate in change.

In the Fast Lane, technology is used to dominate markets, people, and systems. Here is an example. My Ashoka colleague Judit Costa shared news about an Austrian startup, GoStudent, with me. They had closed a 300 million euro investment round to expand their online tutoring for children. But for GoStudent, technology is not an enabler for the people left behind by a broken system. It is the opposite. Technology fuels the anxieties of ambitious parents that their children might not come out on top. With GoStudent they buy private tutoring outside school to help their children gain an edge over other children.

Their parents, in turn, do the same. It is a clever way to create a dynamic market.

The Slow Lane, however, uses technology as an enabler of empowerment. The first story in this chapter, "Playing All the Scales," starts with GoStudent, to explain how Fast Lane technology is synonymous with trying to reach scale as a way to gain dominance. Successful Slow Lane movements practice scale too, but with the purpose of empowering people and strengthening valuable public institutions. Serlo is an example of such an enabling technology, built around inclusive principles that strengthen the quality of learning for all, inside the public school system. In the second story, "An App, or Nothing?" we dive into the power exerted not just through technology but the Fast Lane founders who, as philanthropists, are trying to impose their startup playbook on Slow Lane movements. We explore these power dynamics and how movements withstand the pressure to abandon the complex human relationships they serve for the sake of scale. And our third story, "The Technology of Caring," follows the journey of Dr. Sanjeev Arora, a physician in New Mexico. He created Project ECHO, a global movement and technology platform that makes complex medical treatments accessible to millions of people in remote areas.

The stories of Serlo and Project ECHO show just how powerful an enabler technology can be. While the startup playbook is the source of much philanthropic capital, we cannot disrupt our way out of tackling complex human and social problems. What is needed is a new approach, designed for the long haul.

For this to happen, technologists have to get into the Slow Lane and embrace its principles. This requires what I call a double leap of faith. It means going all the way to empower users to build and control the technology, not just use it. Using technology as an enabler is in fact not a matter of technology. It is a matter of listening and sharing the agency, of nurturing humility, respect, trust, human relationships, and common values. Technologists need to find the humility to see eye-to-eye with the people they hope to empower. All this means that successful Slow Lane movements hold the urgency when it comes to technology too. That's when technology will follow human relationships, instead of manipulating them. At the speed of trust.

Playing All the Scales

In an interview GoStudent founder Felix Ohswald was asked to react to pushback against his private tutoring app. Teachers opposed the idea that education should be commercialized. In response, he argued that education is already commercial, even in places like Germany (where it is free) because taxpayer money pays 12,000 euros per year, per child, to fund it.[1] In his vision of a better future the public education in the morning would be complemented by online private tutoring in the afternoon.

Go (Compete) Student!

GoStudent offers an interesting case when thinking about scale. For startups, scale is everything. Unlike small businesses, startups raise venture capital on the promise that they will disrupt things—and then grab and dominate a large market. A technology startup pitch to an investor includes many ideas about scale. How big is the market? How can we frame the opportunity in a smart way, to maximize its potential? What will it take to dominate the market? How long will it take to get there? How profitable will it be?

Questions, designed to guide all business decisions. It is only from this logic that we can understand the answers offered by Felix Ohswald. He argues that public schools are not providing enough knowledge and that there is a considerable market for online tutoring to fill the gap. Why he would mention the 12,000 euros we pay in taxes for a year of schooling for a child remains unclear. It could be a call to arms for taxpayers, to demand less spending on public schools and more for private tutoring.

Playing with Fire

Here is why I think GoStudent is a dangerous proposition. GoStudent feeds on bad numbers, to serve some of our darkest instincts when it comes to education. Their central claim is that public schools are not feeding enough knowledge to our children. By "enough," they mean that we are not competitive and that others are learning more. Our children will fall behind. It brings to mind a dystopian image of children around the world, competing to outdo one another.

In a GoStudent world parents are in a race to the top. A race in which they compete by cramming as much tutoring into their children as money can buy, in the hope that they come out ahead. This is where the bad numbers come into play. GoStudent plays into a system that makes children compete on standardized skills that are easy to measure (like math or grammar). Then we rank our children in a global race to the top. All this is very problematic because what is left unsaid is that this is a race rigged very much in favor of children of the rich and educated. What is also left unsaid is that in countries like Germany we treat education as a public good, a good that should be available to everyone, on equal terms. Also left unsaid is that young people should have a say about their schooling. And furthermore, that parents buying their children private tutoring in the afternoon to gain an edge over others are less likely to get involved in making public schools better for everyone in the morning.

In short, in a country like Germany, where a free education system struggles to provide equal opportunity and inclusion, GoStudent is set to only deepen inequalities.

Tweaking for Good

"Scale," in and of itself, is a neutral word. It can refer to the pursuit of growth, a proportion, or a scientific truth. The stories in this book show that we can practice scale in meaningful ways, by reframing the world around us, in which those who were considered weak and powerless in the past take charge and create new answers. Dorica Dan used scale creatively to reframe the singular needs of her daughter Oana into a mission to build a care system fit to serve a million people suffering rare diseases. Rebuilding the world around her one child helped Dorica see what could empower the many. And by replicating this caring one-to-one relationship, she built a movement in which other patients like Oana now oversee the government's program for rare diseases. There is no doubt that Dorica wants to go big, but her idea of bigness moves at the speed of empowering each person, according to their complex individual needs and capabilities. Dorica's idea of success is to let every patient create their own care experience and thus contribute to the whole system.

Rosanne's organization, Community Solutions, was designed for scale. Built for Zero wants to end homelessness in America. It is the result of a constant reframing of the problem, inspired by decades of hands-on work with people experiencing homelessness. The campaign is at once visionary and technocratic: Built for Zero prescribes a discipline of counting people, understanding their needs, and solving their individual cases. Community Solutions doesn't actually put people experiencing homelessness in charge of achieving these results. Instead, it is a societal effort to free people from an inhuman condition. That tactic would not make sense in Brownsville, where the goal was never to fix things for people. In this instance, "scale" has a different meaning. United for Brownsville is a racial-equity program first, building on a long tradition of community activism and self-determination going back to the 1960s.

Not So Fast, Please!

How we approach time matters too. Rosanne and Dorica are impatient, pushing hard to grow their national programs. Yet they also appear to be eternally patient when it comes to building the human relationships that empower people to take charge. It is easy to see how doing one without the other would be more convenient. That's how shelters that service, rather than end, homelessness come about. What motivates people to engage at all these different scales, and speeds, is their sensibility for the full journey of empowerment within a larger system.

Fast Lane technology startups like GoStudent, by contrast, often pick the path that narrowly suits their mission and gain. Technology, for them, is a means to dominate others. They are the symptoms of the Fast Lane, in which companies pick the easy path to scale, focusing on the commercially viable parts of our systems for "disruption." They ask, "Why get involved in the messy journey to empowerment by improving public schools, creating places for equity or inclusion, or empowering young people—when you can sell tutoring to their parents?" But as they travel down that path, they risk doing more harm than good. Ride-hailing apps like Uber claimed to offer a quick, convenient fix to congestion, but they've ended up causing traffic jams and sucking passengers and money out of our public transit systems.[2] If Dorica had pursued her cause like GoStudent, she would have developed a premium health-care offering, tailored to the individual needs of wealthy patients.

Empowering One and a Million

For a long time I thought that we had to choose between operating deeply in one community or at a national or global scale.

Dorica and Rosanne show us how we can refuse to accept this choice. They are building a highway for empowerment from the deep, one-to-one relationship all the way up to the corridors of power.

What matters most is a clear sense of who we are solving for. GoStudent, at the end of the day, solves for the very narrow needs of investors. It targets parents who want to elevate their children above others, forcing everyone else to do the same. Wrapped in an easy-to-use app, GoStudent may well meet investor expectations, even if it ends up feeding on the anxieties of families. Young people and professional educators seem to have no real say in the matter. Some successful Slow Lane movements have found a way to maintain a clear sense of who they are solving for *and* use technology to create real pathways for empowerment.

Enter Simon Köhl. Simon is building quite a different type of education technology. He frames the problem differently from the outset: classrooms in Germany struggle to meet the needs of children from socially and culturally diverse backgrounds as well as those with disabilities. According to Simon, there are 453,000 high school students in Germany who are both poor and experience difficulties in school. Simon's approach is to close this learning gap by building a technology platform, Serlo, much like Wikipedia. With Serlo, teachers and students collaborate to curate customized learning experiences.

Learning with Serlo empowers both students and teachers. Students are more actively involved in the classroom, participate in discussion, and contribute to enriching the learning experience. Teachers, for their part, become facilitators who help students personalize learning content and engage in discussion. They also improve the quality of learning content on Serlo. By 2020, ten years after Simon started Serlo as a high school student, 1.5 million students used the platform every month. Serlo's open standards let other nonprofit organizations that want to close the learning gap tap into its offering. Like Chancenwerk, a nonprofit that facilitates a learning cadence of tutoring for students, who in turn offer tutoring to younger students, who go on to do the same for younger students.

Serlo is managed by a hundred volunteers who build the technology, develop content, manage partnerships, and provide support. In 2020, Serlo's annual budget was just 349,000 euros. That's about 0.1 percent of GoStudent's latest investment round. And as of 2022, Serlo is being integrated into Germany's national digital learning infrastructure, to become more accessible to all teachers and classrooms.

An App, or Nothing?

> The biggest critique that FreeFrom gets, almost always
> from people in the tech world, is that we're doing too
> much. We've gotten a lot of pushback that we aren't
> using technology across the board.
>
> **Sonya Passi**

Why of all things would people from the tech world criticize FreeFrom, a nonprofit organization that helps survivors of intimate partner violence by giving them the resources to get safe, heal, and escape future harm?[3] The answer goes right to the heart of the love/hate relationship between the Slow Lane and technology.

The Promised Land

Serlo is the kind of success story that gets the Slow Lane excited about technology: a group of high school students who build a collaborative learning platform, inspired by Wikipedia, that serves 1.5 million students every month on a shoestring budget. Technology, here, makes it possible to serve countless students for free without commercializing their data. Technology spreads the tools for great education experiences, powered by students, teachers, and volunteers. As an organization, Serlo is similar to a workers' cooperative. It is owned by the members of a nonprofit association—teachers, students, contributors—all committed to keeping Serlo free, and free from advertising or other commercial practices. Serlo is transparent about where its money comes from.[4] Decisions aren't made by executives but instead by a plenary of forty-five team members. The whole of Serlo, in short, is designed to empower young people to learn better, both individually and in teams.

Building a piece of technology that is useful to an almost un-limited number of users is a compelling proposition. Movements hope to achieve the kind of network effects that have made Serlo so cost-effective, in which users become volunteers who create more content, which in turn makes Serlo more useful to students and teachers. And like Community Solutions, many Slow Lane movements are interested in data to improve their outcomes. Built for Zero collects "real-time, by name data" to more effectively help every person experiencing homelessness. In another example, The Syrian Archive collects thousands of videos of human rights violations uploaded by people in Syria. It is run by Mnemonic, an NGO that archives and shares this data openly, to support the work of human rights defenders, such as journalists and investigators. Without the efforts of Mnemonic, human rights organizations risk losing vital evidence to the moderation practices of platforms like Facebook or YouTube.

If Only It Wasn't So Hard

We have laws that work against us solving intimate partner violence. I can't create an app to fix that. I've got to engage with the humans. Part of the way that

> intimate partner violence thrives is that it isolates
> people. And it creates such financial devastation, that
> you're unable to engage in your community and your
> society in a way that you once could or would want to.
> I can't create an app for breaking isolation, either.
>
> **Sonya Passi**

Tech holds all these promises, and more.[5] Making it happen, is much harder. And that brings us back to the comments made by Sonya Passi, the founder of FreeFrom, a nonprofit based in Los Angeles that supports survivors of intimate partner violence. Her biggest critics are people from the tech world. Most of the money to fund the costly, and risky, development of technology comes from people who have made it in the tech business. Few Slow Lane movements have the skills that Serlo had to build their own technology. Technology is so costly to develop, in part because programmers are expensive but also because it is so hard to build something that works.

It takes a lot of trial and error to see, for example, if students will use a learning tool. Then it can take a very long time to get enough users to achieve the desired impact. Technology only really becomes cheap once it is very successful. Conventional donors and philanthropists have long preferred to fund predictable projects, guaranteed to help people. That changed when successful tech entrepreneurs looked to bring their experience to the field of social change. They offered a new opportunity to the Slow Lane, bringing enthusiasm and money for tech.

Go All In!

We can work backward from Sonya's case. People from the tech world criticized Sonya because they wanted her to reach more victims, faster. Their instinct was to do what they had done in business: get to scale, fast. Instead of offering a variety of services to survivors of intimate partner violence, they wanted her to pick one service, like providing money, and use technology to make it big. Sonya insisted that this made no sense, when complex human conditions call for holistic care, not a quick fix. Many people from the tech world lose interest at this point. Tech for them is an all-or-nothing game.

Here is how tech investors explained this "all in" logic to me. Tech is incredibly risky, so hard to get right. Unless your organization is "all in," it will not be committed enough to make it work. The result would be a half-baked solution that is at best assistive, instead of transformative. Another way to ensure success in tech is the team. Great people deliver really great results, while average teams are likely to fail. Great tech people, though, aren't interested in working on the sidelines of an organization that also values other things. They want to be the stars in an all-out tech organization. This logic is deeply ingrained in the sector, especially among people who have succeeded in the tech world.

The Truism

But is "all in" true, or a self-fulfilling prophecy? It is true that most organizations that also built an app end up not really transforming the world through their technology or maximize its potential. More inclined to play things safe, they may stop investing when things don't work. The truism, however, is also true. Tech funders will not fund projects that are not "all in," meaning that their money and expertise is simply not available to other, more hybrid projects. Without their commitment, projects end up with less money to get it right and none of their invaluable expertise. And too many great engineers have bought into the same narrative, repeated everywhere. They remain uninterested unless the project is "all in."

What they all fail to see is how Fast Lane success is not a

model for technology to improve society. Sonya doesn't want to pick a problem that technology can solve, or grab market share, or "lock in" survivors of abuse. She wants to empower survivors of abuse, whatever that takes.

It isn't easy to translate the success of projects like Serlo to the wider Slow Lane. They work because they solve a problem that tech can solve in the first place. Serlo also benefits from the school environment, where teachers organize learning around their technology. The same wouldn't hold true for Albina Ruiz's movement to empower waste-pickers in Peru. Tech could have helped her movement organize or even track the implementation of laws more efficiently. But the "all in" question could have had disastrous effects. Betting scarce resources on an app might have destroyed the whole movement. Albina would have seen it as a distraction from the actual work of empowerment. The real question is how technology and data can live up to their promise when complex human needs are involved.

A New Playbook

Until recently, there were really only two playbooks to succeed in technology. One was the open-source movement playbook that at times brought thousands of volunteer contributors together to build an ambitious project, like Wikipedia, Linux, Firefox, or Serlo. The other is the startup playbook, in which a small team takes the risk to create a technology that generates enough excitement to grab and control a market. Along the way, venture capital investors place bets on their success. The startup playbook has famously given us the stars of the Fast Lane like Facebook, Uber, Amazon, and Tesla—with all their negative externalities when it comes to privacy, surveillance, data hoarding, manipulation. What both playbooks have in common, despite their different purposes, is that they are both "all in" and that they rely on people who believe in technology as a solution and want to focus on problems that technology can solve. Predictably, the people in charge of these projects lack diversity. Even Wikipedia suffers from this homogeneity, as the vast majority of articles are authored by men.[6]

Neither playbook responds to the needs of the Slow Lane, where complex human needs often defy tech fixes. Other promising ideas have emerged. They come with names like Public Interest Technology, Civic Tech, and Societal Platforms. What they have in common is a deep commitment to solving not just for the majority but for everyone. And they seek to rectify many of the concerns about Fast Lane technologies. Public Interest Technology, for example, has become a new method to rebuild dysfunctional online services, like benefits or food stamps, delivered by governments and public agencies. Here, teams put people first, involving them to replace overly complex corporate systems with simpler services, designed to the needs of users. Technology here is only a part of what makes a public service successful. In the words of my former colleague Hana Schank, of New America, "digitizing a broken process gets you a digitized, broken process."

Civic Tech caters more to the needs of political and social activists, building tools to organize movements or campaigns, or offering direct services to underserved people. Societal Platforms are a more recent development and have emerged from a movement that promotes digital public goods. The idea of digital public goods is to build a trusted alternative to the dominant platforms like Facebook or Amazon or intrusive government systems. It is the most comprehensive of all playbooks, looking to create truly open systems that serve the public. Real Societal Platforms are open to anyone, as user or contributor, to enable the kind of positive network effects that make Wikipedia or Serlo possible.

Slow Lane Technology?

Taken together, these movements represent a mind-set shift about the role technology should play in social change. They also offer a new resource. This crowd is more diverse than the traditional startup and open-source communities were. And it offers a broader skill-set to understand and solve for human needs. What is emerging is a new community of practice that is not insisting that everyone has to be "all in," but is delighted to contribute in environments that deal with complex human needs.

In early 2020 my colleague Karen Bannan at New America hosted *The Commons Live!*, a webinar to explore how we can deal with technology in the Slow Lane, when technology isn't the only answer.[7] We invited Sonya Passi and Eric Dawson, the founder of Peace First, because both of them work with complex needs of people and are hopeful about technology. We found that technology is never neutral but deeply intertwined with the Fast Lane dynamics of power and domination. That, we agreed, was the real problem to solve.

The Technology of Caring

The answer came to Dr. Sanjeev Arora all at once, in a morning meditation. For years he had witnessed patients who suffer from hepatitis C—an infectious disease that targets the liver—come to his clinic in Albuquerque, New Mexico, too late for treatment. At the time, twenty-eight thousand people suffered from hepatitis C in New Mexico. And only fifteen hundred received the specialist treatment needed to cure the disease. Wherever Sanjeev went, he heard the same story: local doctors didn't have the expertise required to treat the disease. And patients simply couldn't travel for hours to his clinic.

For a while, Sanjeev had unsuccessfully attempted to get

hepatitis C treatment to people in remote areas by sharing his treatment protocols with doctors in rural areas. But something different was needed. In his daily meditation Sanjeev kept coming back to the question of how he could make a difference. That's how, one day, the whole answer came to him, an answer that would help Sanjeev and thousands of others make a real difference. The idea became Project ECHO, an open-source community that uses online video conferencing to share expert knowledge and skills. It started in 2003 in New Mexico, when primary care providers met in video conferences to learn how to treat hepatitis C by working through individual cases with experts like Sanjeev.

I first met Sanjeev in 2012, nine years after he started Project ECHO. At the time, ECHO was considered a big success, reaching more than five thousand learners in eight countries. By 2021 that number had grown to seven hundred thousand learners in almost two hundred countries, bringing complex skills, like hepatitis C treatments, to more than ten thousand cities. Project ECHO even brought the expertise for treating the rare Prader-Willi syndrome to Dorica's remote province in Romania. The ECHO model proved useful in making all kinds of complex nonmedical education accessible. The Albuquerque Police Department uses ECHO to train officers on crisis intervention. In prisons it offers mentoring programs. Teachers of young children use ECHO to access mental health and other teaching resources.

Not a Technology, but a Network of Care

When we reconnected in 2021, Sanjeev told me that too many people mistake ECHO for a technology. And it is true, ECHO is an impressive open-source platform using ever more sophisticated technologies like Artificial Intelligence to assist learning. But to Sanjeev, the technology is secondary. The real star at

ECHO are the values that underpin its mission, what motivates people to join. It is essentially a giving network, powered by human relationships.

First, I train you. Then you train others. That basically sums up how ECHO works. How you do that matters a lot to Sanjeev. He realized early on that many nonprofits failed to succeed in bringing about really large-scale change because they stopped focusing on their mission to change things and instead focused on sustaining themselves. Nonprofits like this essentially serve two masters: their mission for change and their own organizational (mostly financial) needs.

Disruptively Open

To avoid this, Sanjeev developed a set of principles to guide his decisions. The first was about intellectual property. Many nonprofit medical institutions and universities guard the knowledge they create and then sell it to generate income. ECHO would insist that all knowledge and technology is open, shared freely the day it is created. This also applied to the recognition Sanjeev himself received for his pioneering work: he gave all awards and fellowships to ECHO. His personal income, he insists, is limited to his regular position at the university. He felt that if he didn't lead by example, financial incentives would gradually undermine the openness of the ECHO network.

By 2021 the US government had invested more than a billion dollars into projects related to ECHO. With all its success, large funds offered to buy out ECHO. Others wanted to partner to offer corporate training services. At one point a Harvard Business School professor tried to mentor Sanjeev, to develop a sustainable business model. No one seemed to be able to get their head around ECHO's principle of never charging. In Sanjeev's mind, the minute you charge, you inevitably take care away from the poorest. That would undermine his personal mission, to help six billion underserved people. Sanjeev worries about how the triangle of monetization, sustainability, and personal wealth can undermine our missions.

ECHO has a very forward position when it comes to money. It doesn't charge any fees for accessing the model or the technology. The rule is simply that if you want to help people, you can use ECHO. Fifty-five thousand partner organizations do just that, and they have no obligations to share their grant money with ECHO. Technically speaking, the partner organizations often end up competing with Sanjeev for grant funding. This dynamic, no-strings-attached model has led to ECHO's rapid growth and attracted scientific interest in its own right. More than three hundred research papers have studied the ECHO model, independently demonstrating its effectiveness.[8] This made partnering with ECHO a popular way to raise grant funding, incentivizing more medical institutions to join and open up their knowledge. As a result, a university hospital may come to ECHO to gain an edge on a grant application or to improve local health outcomes.

Tech to Hold the Flywheel of Openness

This rapid growth began to put a strain on ECHO's simple operational model. In essence, all it did was use Zoom conference calls to organize the communities of practice. People loved learning and contributing in this way, but it began to become unmanageable. Sanjeev felt that he was at a crossroads. Either their growth would stagnate, following their past model. Or they could go into uncharted territory, sacrificing certainty to move forward. In 2019, encouraged by the opportunity of technology, Sanjeev and the team at ECHO set a new goal: to reach a billion people by 2025. Despite their success so far, they wanted to make a difference on the really big picture, where a child diagnosed with cancer in Africa has just five years of life expectancy, compared to twenty years in America.

Key to achieving this goal is ECHO Digital, an upgrade to the original open-source technology. Sanjeev was inspired to embark on this journey by a conversation with Nandan Nilekani, one of India's most successful technology entrepreneurs and a committed philanthropist. They shared an understanding that ECHO was a societal platform—a human network first, not software. In their thinking, it is the human network that makes the technology more effective, not the other way around. ECHO Digital is a bet to lower the barriers to entry, and amplify the impact of what is already going on. Sanjeev is confident that twenty years after launching Project ECHO, the community has deepened its culture to a point where technology can play a bigger role without undermining their relationships and values. Users will have a better experience, and knowledge will be captured more effectively, which in turn will make ECHO better for everyone. And more affordable.

A Technology of Love and Kindness

"I focus 100 percent on values," Sanjeev says in our conversation. He returns to what connects everyone, and everything, in what ECHO does. Searching for his calling in life, Sanjeev meditated on the primary purpose of life: love and kindness. These values are inextricable from ECHO and the global infrastructure it now provides to millions. Like Serlo, ECHO builds on the traditions of open-source movements, ensuring not just that infrastructures are open but a wariness of how personal and organizational financial needs can misguide a mission for change. Technology was always central to ECHO, starting with the first video-conferencing apps. But it was never more than an enabler for relationships, to bridge physical distance. Or as he likes to say, to move knowledge, not people.

To me, ECHO is proof that you don't have to be "all in" to make good use of technology. Sanjeev took it slow as he waited for the right kind of technologist to help take ECHO forward. Someone who wouldn't impose a Fast Lane playbook on a human network of care. What attracts people to join ECHO isn't technology. It is the power and generosity of human relationships, of caring, learning, and mentoring. ECHO is an infrastructure, effective at sharing even complex know-how, with the best of human values engineered right into it.

Hey Techies, Get in the Slow Lane!

In 2009, I met Boris in Stockholm. Elisabeth Harsanji, a project manager at a small digital mapping company called Astando, had arranged the meeting. Boris was blind. And Boris told me about how, thanks to a small navigation aid developed by Astando, he could now go anywhere in Stockholm without assistance. In his words, he was truly free for the first time in his life. No need to ask for help to go anywhere. I have written and spoken for years about this transformative solution, called e-Adept.[9]

To get it just right, e-Adept was developed in a remarkable collaboration between Astando, the City of Stockholm, and three hundred visually impaired citizens, including Boris. They nailed it. Boris was very satisfied, ready to start what amounted to a new life for him. Project managers at city hall loved the technology because, according to their impact models, it promised to save 16 million euros a year. And then e-Adept got canceled because there was "no sustainable business model" to be found. Boris eventually had to start asking for help again every time he wanted to leave the house.

For years now I have chewed on the fate of e-Adept. Why did a brilliant technology that truly transformed lives fail? I played through different scenarios: What if the team had raised venture capital, to get it right? Or had built an open-source movement to let anyone assemble their own e-Adept, use it, improve it, and share the results? But neither of these paths were viable for two reasons. The first was infrastructure. No other city but Stockholm had the kind of high-quality, real-time data on streets and roadworks that made e-Adept possible. Any effort to use e-Adept in other cities would have had to not just build technology for the blind but lobby city halls everywhere to make serious upgrades to their data infrastructure. Moreover, there was no entrepreneurial leader or movement to back e-Adept. While the people in charge saw Boris and his peers as co-creators, they had no real power. To those leading the project, Boris was simply a passive consumer of public services.

Because there was no place for it in the Fast Lane, e-Adept failed. It also failed because it wasn't anchored in the Slow Lane. Neither the commercial market, nor the return-on-investment mind-set in government, was able to make sense of it. Looking back, I wish we had known about how students built their own classroom technology with Serlo. It would have shown us that trying to crack e-Adept's technical and financial problems overlooked the much bigger issue: it had occurred to nobody that co-creating the project with users was never going to be enough. Users like Boris should have owned it. Because for e-Adept to really work, Stockholm would have had to change how it delivers care services. And there is no way this happens, unless there is sustained pressure from the people who have everything to gain. In short: Boris and his peers should have been asked to take charge and keep up the pressure. That's why Dorica helped rare disease patients get a seat on the national reform council in Romania—with voting rights.

The Double Leap of Faith

In Stockholm, city managers had left their comfort zone when they involved visually impaired people in the design of e-Adept.

Designers had rightly convinced them that users should be involved in developing such a transformative technology. Boris was the real expert when it came to his needs. What they missed was the opportunity that Serlo and Project ECHO saw: that they could go all the way, when it comes to empowerment. High-school students don't just use technology, they can build and control it, leading to powerful changes in thousands of classrooms.

Dr. Sanjeev Arora had similar trust in the capabilities of small-town medical professionals. Why shouldn't they be able to treat hepatitis C and then teach others what they learned? Stockholm would have stood a much greater chance of transforming thousands of lives and saving millions of euros if they had done the double leap, to real empowerment. Instead of building technology for the people, it should have been built *by* the people. This is what applying the principle of sharing the agency to technology looks like.

Patient Code

Technology startups typically chase the tipping point, at which they have the critical mass to reap the profits of network effects or large-scale adoption of their technology. Their race to the top is fraught with attempts to find shortcuts to get there faster. Companies like Uber or WeWork have sunk billions to effectively pay customers for using their service, or simply give it away for free. Facebook let hate speech and manipulative algorithms fester for fear of slowing down growth.

ECHO took a different path to growth, one in which the technology simply followed the network of human relationships that Sanjeev seeded. Hundreds of thousands of people already adhered to the values and practices promoted by ECHO *before* it became more automated. Fifty-five thousand partner institutions help control quality and help replicate the community values. By any standard, ECHO and Serlo are spectacular successes, without having to use aggressive tactics to take control of their markets.

How they pay for technology matters too. In 2018 it cost Serlo less than one-tenth to support a student than it costs Facebook to serve a single user. And unlike Facebook, Serlo provides high-quality content. Serlo is so much cheaper to operate because volunteers contribute a lot. More important, it doesn't spend tens of billions of dollars on marketing and buying up competitors every year, to pursue further control of the market. Funded by a nonprofit association of people who contribute and benefit from Serlo, it has found a healthy balance that doesn't rely on fast growth. And it doesn't see other offers, like Khan Academy, as competitors but as part of an open system. Financial transparency and shared decision-making in the team discourage acting on impulse or placing big bets; frugality is promoted instead.

While ECHO is a much bigger animal than Serlo, it is also exceptionally cost-effective from Sanjeev's perspective. Hundreds of thousands of professional contributors are funded by their universities, through grant money for research or through care services enabled by learning new skills with ECHO. Sanjeev estimates that to operate ECHO, he needs to raise less than 5 percent of the actual cost of ECHO. Remember, he doesn't charge anyone for using the platform! All this means that Serlo and ECHO can build technology without having to achieve artificial growth targets, which would distract them from putting healthy human relationships first.

Will a Bot Put Us All into the Slow Lane?

My friend Dr. Anthony Townsend at Cornell Tech challenged me to imagine a world where robots and AI take care of our menial care tasks, allowing us to spend more time building movements and practicing social imagination together. Could this kind of automation free humanity up to spend more time in the Slow Lane?

I prefer to frame this scenario differently. Technology may or may not free up more of our time. And we may or may not use that freedom to look after one another. But what the Slow Lane shows us is that technology can enable more people to contribute. That's what excited me about seeing Boris walk the streets of Stockholm. e-Adept empowered Boris to become a truly active citizen, engaged in work, tourism, culture, and politics. And in the Slow Lane. Serlo and ECHO aren't about freeing up time. They bring knowledge and know-how to where it is needed most, empowering new people to create their own solutions.

It's Time to Put Techies at the Service of Real Change!

Funders, technologists, designers, and regulators building technology for good should understand how the Slow Lane works. While the startup playbook is the source of much philanthropic capital, we cannot pivot or disrupt our way out of tackling the complex human and social "always" problems. What is needed is a new approach, designed for the long haul.

Using technology as an enabler requires what I call a double leap of faith. It means going all the way to empower users to build and control the technology, not just use it. It is in fact not a matter of technology at all. Instead, it pulls together all other Slow Lane Principles: It is a matter of having the humility to hold the urgency. It is to listen to build trust. It is to share the agency, to empower users to take charge. And it is to nurture curiosity, to unlearn the old technology playbooks and let a new formula take shape.

It is only when techies have the humility to truly see eye to eye with the people they hope to empower that we can put technology at the service of social change. At the speed of trust.

= 6 =

Heal Democracy

Today, we as a people have spoken. And we say that
we trust women and we respect women and their
decisions....Our democracy is vibrant and robust
and can survive divisive debate and make difficult
decisions.

Taoiseach Leo Vardkar

This chapter is about how we can apply the Slow Lane
Principles to heal our democracies. The Fast Lane, in its pursuit of quick fixes and domination, breeds division in our communities. Some of these are intentional, like the divisive identity politics promoted by populist politicians. Others happen
almost unwittingly and are deeply engrained in the systems
by which we build technology or deliver services. Like the
fact that according to Raul Krauthausen, a German disability
activist, most electric vehicle charging stations in Europe are
inaccessible to wheelchair users.[1] It appears that no engineer
had thought about people with disabilities, when they developed their ideas for a clean energy revolution in transportation.

Two stories help us see how Slow Lane movements can
heal our divisions, and by extension our democracies. The

first story, "The Day I Met Yuraima Taught Me All There Is to Know," takes us to Venezuela, a country that has been in freefall since the late 1990s. We follow the story of Yuraima Martín and other activists in Catuche, a slum in the capital city of Caracas, where a decades-long effort has been under way to give people self-determination to take charge of their destiny—against all odds. In "In·valu·able: Precious Beyond Measure," we follow Denisa Livingston and the families in the Navajo Nation who fight a diabetes epidemic and a long history of oppression by reimagining their food system, drawing on long-lost traditions. Their latest wins on a journey that spans generations: the first junk food tax and a thousand well-being projects. Along the way, women and girls get a real taste of power.

Slow Lane movements strengthen our democracy. They sidestep not just the quick fixes but also the quick wins that, although cheap to obtain, cause lasting division and pain. Slowing down to practice social imagination is a powerful defense to protect us from divisive forces.

The Day I Met Yuraima Taught Me All There Is to Know

Caracas, 1996. Looking back now, almost everything I ever needed to know happened the day I met Yuraima Martín. Far away from my home in London, I had rumbled through the mad traffic of Caracas, the capital of Venezuela, on a mini-bus, and from there by spanking clean metro to reach the campus of the Central University of Venezuela. Built by the architect Carlos Raul Villanueva in the early 1950s, the campus is a masterpiece of modernist design in Latin America. It is in fact my personal favorite piece of architecture anywhere in the world. A beautiful place to learn, with classrooms opening into lush gardens and dogs sleeping in the shade of tropical trees, the campus is filled with colorful sculptures and murals by local and international artists, including Fernand Léger and Alexander Calder.

All this art and architecture came together as a vision for a country on the move, to a bright future for all. What had brought me to Venezuela, however, wasn't its visionary architecture. In 1996 it was very far from the hopeful vision crafted forty years earlier. It was on the edge. Its broken, unjust, and discriminatory political system was on the brink of collapse. A country that holds the largest known oil reserves in the world was drowning in inequality, injustice, and violence. And Caracas was the battleground, with 70 percent of the population living in informal settlements. In slums.

The university campus was the first stop on my trip, and I came here to meet Yuraima Martín, a young professor of architecture. She was also an activist who, together with many other academics, was trying to assist the development of slums in Caracas in a new way. I was interested in these slums because they are a testament to discriminatory public policies and represent immense human resilience and ingenuity. Many great architects and planners had tried to intervene in slums. They had all failed, revealing the vanity of their projects. As an architecture student, it seemed to me that if I wanted to understand the essence of what architecture can contribute to society, the slums of Caracas would be a good place to start. And so my professors had pointed me to Yuraima and her colleagues.

Looking into Trouble

What had first inspired me to travel to Caracas was my visit, a year earlier, to Soweto—the largest township in South Africa. Following the election of Nelson Mandela, social and political activists in South Africa had been riding the wave of triumph, liberation, and their mandate for change. Venezuela, in 1996, was nothing like this. The country was stuck in its own version of apartheid, where instead of outright racism, the discrimination was against the poor. In Venezuela there was nothing like the political movement or activism of the African National Congress or the international sanctions against South Africa to push for change.

In Venezuela change was not in the air. Internationally it was best known for its oil, soap operas (telenovelas), and beauty queens. Those most acutely suffering from the state of affairs were the 37 percent of Venezuelans who were living in extreme poverty and more than 60 percent in informal settlements.[2] They were systematically deprived of citizenship, voting rights, and access to public services. Here the cards were firmly stacked against change.

Caracas was a city that worked only for the most privileged people. As an oil-rich country practicing social discrimination, its capital served the needs of the wealthy and their cars first. Without a car, it was literally impossible to get around neighborhoods crisscrossed by motorways. People who lived in informal settlements had no cars and therefore little means to use the city. When you looked at the city from above, it was a spectacular lesson in social geography: modern high-rise buildings, parks, and civic buildings occupied flat areas. All else, the precarious hillsides prone to landslides were built up with huts, some of them stacked ten or more stories high. This segregation and injustice was unsustainable. By 1996, Caracas was the world's most dangerous city. Its murder rate was only comparable to that of an active war zone.[3]

The Place That Taught Me Everything

Yuraima had followed in her father César's footsteps to become an architect. Where other academics were supporting the informal settlements at arm's length from their faculties and homes in the privileged areas of Caracas, Yuraima and César had chosen to live and work in Catuche, a slum right in the heart of the city. Their vision was not just to provide technical assistance but to be of service. In this, they were a lot like the Jesuits, who had moved to the area decades earlier to run schools as well as social and community services. And so, the first thing we did, upon meeting on the beautiful grounds of the university, was to leave for Catuche and enter Yuraima and César's world.

Yuraima parked her car on one of the regular streets just outside Catuche. From here we followed a spidery network of steep stairs, passageways, and bridges to enter the neighborhood with its impossible geography, home to eleven thousand people. It was a labyrinth of houses organized around the Catuche creek that comes down from the Avila mountains and gives the community its name. For more than a hundred years it had brought drinking water from the mountains into the city. Now, in the absence of municipal services, it served as a place for people to dispose of their human and material waste. The creek was a black, smelly source of disease. We met families, children, gang members, and community organizers.

This settlement had started over fifty years earlier, and yet official documents denied its existence because no official had ever granted permission for its existence. In a cynical reminder of Venezuela's discriminatory politics, maps at the planning office showed nothing but trees where Catuche stood. Eleven thousand people with all their lives and shelter were simply invisible to the bureaucrats. In Catuche, like the country as a whole, the government had for generations systematically not issued birth certificates to poor people in informal settlements. Without citizenship, they were deprived of voting rights, rights to health care, education, and basic municipal services. The political elite had simply declared all twenty million of those in similar informal settlements as "illegal immigrants."

To See the Revolution, You Have to Unlearn

Yuraima showed me the plans for the upgrade of Catuche. At first glance, they did not excite me. I was disappointed. The plans were very sensible, practical engineering measures to secure the area and manage flood water. I had secretly hoped to see some inspiring architecture, new forms, and a grand vision emerge from the unplanned, unregulated life. My outlook changed, however, as I observed the way things worked in Catuche over the coming months. Listening to the life stories and history of people in the area, it dawned on me that in judging the plan, I had overlooked the real sensation.

Here in Catuche, I was witnessing something truly innovative, if not revolutionary. Yuraima and César weren't simply working for the community; they had taken a cue from the Jesuits, who had long ago committed themselves to helping the people of Catuche take charge of their destiny. The Jesuit organization Fe y Alegría had operated in Catuche for decades. Father José Virtuoso, known as Joseito, and Doris Barrento, a longtime community organizer running the community center, were pillars of the community. Together with Yuraima and César, they had spent more than thirty years in the community. Their vision was not so much to help the community, as to provide the community with the care, skills, and resources to help itself.

They had a radical vision: The people of Catuche, after generations of neglect, should be completely emancipated. They should gain full control over all resources invested in their community. Yuraima explained their major achievement to me at the time: The community had negotiated to get 25 million bolivars (about US$250,000 in today's money) in development funding from the municipal government to implement its infrastructure upgrade program as it sees fit. The community was free to determine how to use the money. Someone said that if they wanted to blow it all on a Michael Jackson concert, they could!

A Healing Journey to Empowerment

It had taken years of collaboration with countless organizations to provide the scientific basis and technical assistance needed to achieve this degree of self-determination. It took five years alone to constitute a legal entity fully controlled by the community in 1994, the Consorcio Catuche, to represent their interests and manage the use of development funds. Meanwhile, it was the presence and services offered by the Jesuits—the school, community center, and social activities—that kept bringing people of all ages together. Slowness was a matter of constant debate and negotiation. Do we really need to make decisions in this complicated way and insist on having full control over the funds? Everyone knew that things would have been quicker if they had let government officials do their thing.

But as the project advanced, so did the ability of the community to embrace its complexity. The consortium learned every step of the way and echoed that learning in the community to refine their decisions. Improvements began to happen as they upgraded infrastructure and invested in education and other social measures. With every year the community got stronger. Catuche was not a community advised by expert consultants but a community that was actively winning its right to self-determination. Yuraima, César, Joseito, and Doris were intentionally present in the community. Days weren't organized into meetings but one long conversation moving from door to door, corner to corner. It was a radical departure from what I expected great architecture to look like.

I was reminded of the story of Chandigarh, the new city built to represent India's independence and self-determination.

The government had hired the Swiss-French superstar architect Le Corbusier, the biggest name in architecture of his time, to lead its design. Despite the vision for democracy and independence, the Swiss architect and his colleagues began to sideline their Indian colleagues in decisions to impose their grand ideas. This imposition produced not just indignation among Indian architects but also housing unsuitable to Indian lifestyles. It was criticized for serving the aesthetic aspirations of upper-caste Indians versed in Western culture, instead of society in all its diversity.[4]

What I saw in Catuche was an entirely different approach. Yuraima and César practiced architecture to empower people who had been imposed upon, lied to, cheated, traumatized, and excluded for generations. In Catuche architecture let people experience power for the first time, and they learned how to wield it. What had seemed to be a boring infrastructure plan now looked infinitely more radical and visionary than Le Corbusier's grand schemes! And it would pay off in unexpected ways, as tragic events would unfold in and around Catuche in the years to come.

Design with Truth, Build with Beauty
(in a Failing Country)

Just three years after my stay, in 1999, the Tragedy of Vargas struck Venezuela. Torrential rain caused landslides, killing thousands of people in and around Caracas. Catuche, with the creek running through it, was devastated. Five thousand people lost their homes.[5] Twelve people died. The death toll and destruction would have been much higher if it hadn't been for years of infrastructure upgrades, preparation, and training by the Consorcio Catuche. Everyone knew what to do, how to help. Even the *malandros* (gang members) put their guns aside to help. But the catastrophe set back the community development efforts. Reconstruction was delayed by years, and just as work got under way, the government put a break on it. The government agency responsible for funding the reconstruction work had decided to challenge the Consorcio Catuche's legitimacy and autonomy to implement projects. It took a supreme court challenge by the people of Catuche to assert their right to citizen participation and their right to obtain and control the recovery funding.

After the Tragedy of the Vargas, Venezuela entered a decade of improvements, fueled by a windfall from high oil prices. The country moved from eighty-second place in 2000 to sixty-sixth place in the Human Development Index ranking of 191 countries by 2011.[6] What followed was a rapid descent into deeper and deeper economic, social, and political crisis. From 2011 to 2021, Venezuela's GDP collapsed from $350 billion to $40 billion, and Human Rights Watch issued an alert in 2019 that Venezuela's health care and food systems had collapsed.[7] By 2021 it ranked only 120th place in the Human Development Index. In Catuche, after an endless series of setbacks caused by the political chaos in the country, the Consorcio Catuche was dissolved and replaced by ASOCICA, a new entity controlled entirely by the community that kept the model running.

Operating for thirty years now, this form of organizing and empowerment has succeeded in holding the community together and enabling it to build its capacity to solve problems. As it did in 2005, when mothers from rivaling gang-controlled areas of Catuche hosted a peace summit to stop the chronic violence and killing among their children. Their peace program, facilitated by Doris, held for fourteen years according to reports, a peace that to my knowledge continued to hold into 2022, making gun violence in Catuche a problem of the past.[8]

Catuche stepped out of the hamster wheel of dependence that for generations had trapped it in the hope for the next big project to deliver relief. Despite the hardships and injustices that Catuche has had to endure, the community continued to pursue its vision for improvements. In March 2021, I talked to Maria Isabel Pena, a professor of architecture at the Central University of Venezuela and co-curator of the research consortium CCS450 about Catuche. She told me just how special Catuche remains to this day, with the community now focusing its efforts on developing shared spaces.[9] And as in the spectacular university campus, art is now integral to all new community projects in Catuche. By taking charge, the people of Catuche developed the kind of strength, capabilities, and resilience that helped them to come out stronger even as Venezuela entered into freefall.

Really, Catuche Taught Me All I Needed to Know

Catuche shows how the Slow Lane Principles can work even when we face horrific circumstances. The community succeeded in developing its participatory decision-making against the background of national decline all around it. Instead of everyone fending for their own at a time of crisis, people doubled down as a community, investing in shared spaces, peacemaking, and shared institutions. The people of Catuche came out stronger, more peaceful, and dignified than the rest of the country.

The months I spent in Catuche provided me with three big lessons that changed my values—and my career. First, it helped me unlearn my preconceptions about professional excellence, away from imagining success solely as my ability to impose my ideas on others and toward what I now understand as the third Slow Lane Principle: share the agency. Promoting self-determination centered on the idea that everyone is an expert at their life but also that there is a deeper healing power in letting people contribute their skills and experience after generations of neglect. This was radically different from how Le

Corbusier imposed his vision on Chandigarh. Catuche gained something much more valuable than a masterful piece of architecture: people who take pride and responsibility in imagining and building their dream.

The second lesson I took from Catuche is what I wrote about holding the urgency in Chapter 1. Catuche showed me that we need to do more than slow down a bit here and there. We need to stay for as long as it takes. Catuche is not a project. The work of Yuraima and César, Father Joseito, and Doris and their organization Fe y Alegría have provided continuity, humanity, and care over the course of decades. Especially in precarious communities—wherever people are disadvantaged, poor, stigmatized, struggle to survive, live in fear, are excluded, or not being heard—this kind of permanence is critical. It is easy to be the traveling expert, as I have been throughout my career, diving in and out of communities. The Slow Lane teaches us that we need people and institutions to stay. Holding the urgency in this way is not about leading the community. It is to be of service and provide continuity at difficult moments, when things might otherwise break apart.

The third lesson is about listening. Catuche applied the second Slow Lane Principle in the best possible way. Listening here is open, patient, and generous. And it produces the kind of infrastructure and capacity that, even as Venezuela descended into dictatorship, nurtured a healthy and resilient microcosm of democratic self-determination.

In·valu·able: Precious Beyond Measure

In 2011 the nine-year-old girl stepped up. I never found out her name, but she was suffering from type 2 diabetes, like so many other children and grown-ups in her community. Nine years old and already suffering from a chronic lifestyle disease, one you don't contract by infection but from the way you live. When

I was nine, I only knew of old people suffering lifestyle diseases after decades of unhealthy fatty diets, alcohol, or tobacco use. How can a young girl get diabetes? She might reply, "Welcome to the Navajo Nation," the tribal territory established by the US government to return some control and dignity to Indigenous people after centuries of injustice.

A Hard Truth in a Child's Purse

She might also add that it wasn't her fault. It was hard to get healthy food in the Navajo Nation (also referred to as the Diné Nation)—in fact, 99 percent of the Navajo Nation is classified as a food desert.[10] And there was an inexplicable 6 percent tax on water and fresh food like fruits and vegetables. A tax on healthy food, in a food desert. The Navajos were traditionally healthy and food sovereign, but historical oppression, displacement, internment, and the contamination of tribal lands all contributed to the dramatic decline of traditional food systems. Children now grew up in places where stores sold mainly processed and junk food, with minimal to no nutritional value. It is not surprising that diabetes had become an epidemic, on track to affect seven out of ten people. A nine-year-old in the Navajo Nation never stood a fair chance to avoid the illness.

It Takes a Special Kind of Tribe to Step Up

So she stepped up. She gathered her courage and stood up in front of the Navajo Nation Tribal Council and opened her purse to show them what she carried. A diabetes kit. She asked the Tribal Council to help her and her community. Wasn't it an emergency if children like her got sick? A girl in need of a diabetes kit, however compact, had to be the end of the line for incremental progress. Among other ideas, she proposed that the Tribal Council remove the 6 percent tax on healthy food. And instead put a tax on junk food.

For three years, the young girl returned to the Tribal Council until it removed the tax on healthy food and in 2014 passed the Healthy Diné Nation Act.[11] This made the Tribal Council of the Navajo Nation the first government in the United States to put a 2 percent tax on junk food. The law promotes healthier lifestyles and diets, stipulating that proceeds of the tax have to be invested in community health programs. It had raised $7.5 million by 2021, funding more than a thousand well-being projects led by community members, including hiking trails, playgrounds, greenhouses, cooking classes, traditional food education, and youth participation projects.[12] Furthermore, the government rolled out food voucher programs specifically for fruit and vegetables, to encourage stores to stock more healthy food.

As a proposition, the tax proposal was both compelling and sophisticated. It takes a village, or in this case a tribe, to produce such a proposition. The young girl didn't act alone. She was supported by her family. Her family in turn was part of a movement with countless other families. Holding the alliance together was the job of Denisa Livingston, a local activist and organizer of the Diné Community Advocacy Alliance. Together, they learned about public health, about how to change laws and taxes. They worked together to change their lives to become healthier because a tax alone wouldn't keep diabetes away. And like this movement, communities everywhere are becoming better and better at creating such compelling alternatives. They don't shy away from problems and are not afraid to act or to take ownership.

The NeighborOrganizerScientistStewardEmpowererAncestor

Even through the keyhole perspective of a Zoom call, Denisa projects a boldness of vision and carries her vibrant community right into our conversation. It was 2021. One minute we admired the colorful variety of her family's ancient corn harvest, the next she shared pictures of Covid-19 hygiene kits the Diné Community Advocacy Alliance had produced, when government offices stopped functioning. Denisa channels a constant flow of ideas, people, issues, traditions, support, politics, and science into a movement for empowerment and health. She doesn't own or control this movement, but it would be hard to imagine it without her. Denisa is part of a tradition of community leaders who are deeply connected locally and globally in real time. Regular exchanges with peers from around the world help her hone her skills and tactics.

Denisa is much more than an activist seeking a legislative win. She speaks with an intimacy she has with the families in her community. She is always there for them. In this, she is not unlike Yuraima, César, Doris, and Father Joseito in Catuche. They too have lived and worked in a way that is deeply embedded in the community—for decades. This permanence builds trust and enables them to embody a bigger journey. Denisa says that she is a steward for a much broader vision for change, never taking her eyes off the deeper injustices that her community needs to right.

Denisa describes her work on food systems as nurturing a social gastronomy. As the Slow Food movement's Indigenous counselor for the Global North, she is part of a community that tries to restore traditional food systems and relationships with people, plants, and animals around the world. Denisa says that her journey started generations ago, when her grandmother fought contamination through government-sponsored, unprotected uranium mining. Denisa carries on the work, as she reclaims contaminated land to revive traditional food practices. In her mind the organizing efforts will be passed on for generations to come, always grounding their Slow Lane movement in the wisdom of ancestors and the needs of future generations.

Servant Leadership to Heal Democracy

From the moment I first met Denisa, she struck a deep chord in me. Almost thirty years after Yuraima turned my expectations of excellence on its head, I felt the same sensation. Three thousand miles from the urban slum in Caracas, Denisa's community organizing was not just improving health outcomes but also decolonizing a community and healing democracy. She is leading her movement not by telling them what to do, or where to go, but by providing permanence and by being of service. Her service is to help people find their role in an eternal struggle, to build up their courage, nurture an identity. Some will step up to be the movement's drivers, others will be copilots or passengers. There is no judgment in her saying this. Denisa takes pride in curating these different roles as equals, from speaking up at the Tribal Council to posting a support video on TikTok.

Community organizers like Denisa succeed when they balance whatever urgent battle mobilizes the community right now, with a long-term mission. Providing continuity in this way is an important element of applying the first Slow Lane Principle: hold the urgency. In Denisa's movement the actions always contain a strong undercurrent to restore justice, confidence, identity, ecosystems, traditions, and community. They will simply not do things or behave in ways that undermine the long-term mission. To hold the urgency in this way energizes democracy by aligning with a much wider sea change that is under way. This has led to more and more Indigenous women gaining positions of power in the Navajo Nation. And this in turn unlocks the third Slow Lane Principle: share the agency. In 2020 a record three Native American women got elected to the US Congress.[13] Social change always involves a change in power structures, and Denisa's movement restores a long tribal tradition of involving women in decision-making.

Despite this progress, women (and girls) continue to struggle to be heard by the Navajo Nation Council, where in 2021
just two of twenty-four members were women. Most members
prefer to listen to the incumbent (mostly male) lobbyists. To
make things more equitable, Denisa's movement reinvigorates
a long tradition of sharing power, by helping women and girls
reimagine their roles and reclaim power. One important tool
to achieve this is to apply the fourth Slow Lane Principle: nurture curiosity. The Diné Community Advocacy Alliance taps
into global knowledge gained by other movements every day to
refine their goals and tactics and put them into practice. This
form of learning, and trial and error, lets them experience success, hone their skills, and develop sophisticated plans. Plans
like the Healthy Diné Nation Act that due to its successful implementation was reauthorized in 2020 by resolution CD-96-20
of the Navajo Nation Council.

In·valu·able:
Something So Precious That One Cannot Put a Price to It

As I listen to Denisa and follow her journey, I am reminded of
how universal the Slow Lane Principles of holding the urgency,
listening, and nurturing curiosity are. She says that her movement is very conscious that data, information, and relationships
should always move at the speed of trust. It is a very intentional
approach to sophisticated questions of using information to enable her community to take a leading role.

I wonder how we might ever put a value on a movement
like the Diné Community Advocacy Alliance. Think of all
that it does: It provides an invaluable infrastructure to make
democracy more inclusive. It mobilizes a community around
transformative ideas for a better future, against all odds. It nur-
tures families through an endless series of setbacks, to retain

hope on the long journey toward change. It serves the community with empathy and compassion, building tight personal bonds. It helps out when public institutions fail. It supports Indigenous culture and public health, creating public goods desired by families and the government alike. It draws on science and knowledge to develop constructive ideas that people can act on. And, last but not least, it propels families, and in particular women and girls, into believing in their ability to change things and gain power.

This movement is simply invaluable. To the community, the government, and democracy.

And the Winner Is: Democracy

Navajo women and girls win a voice in community health. Citizens rewrite the Irish constitution after the trauma of the 2008 crash of the Celtic Tiger. Ex-offenders help ex-offenders to help the government reduce reoffending. Waste-pickers help the ministers write laws that will put Peru on a path to a zero-waste society. Sefton's leaders invest in its citizens to help each other thrive. Slum-dwellers in Caracas organize to develop their community.

One big winner in all these stories is democracy. The Slow Lane is full of imaginative ideas for the future that may or may not come to fruition. But in the process, applying the Slow Lane Principles produces incredible value to our democracies. Organizing communities in this way enables people who have long been excluded to participate. Democracies become stronger when more people vote, participate in government and civic life, access quality community services, make peace, build their lives, share their views, help create meaningful laws, and invent creative ways to tackle problems. And democracy becomes richer and more resilient against attempts to divide communities.

The #Wins

Until I began working in the United States in 2015, I had never heard the expression "win." All of a sudden, it seemed that everyone around me was chasing wins. Nonprofits, think tanks, activists, political parties, community organizers, businesses. I soon learned what a "win" is. You have a win when you get something your way. A candidate you backed gets elected to office? Win. The *New York Times* mentions your talking point? Win. The government passes a law you want? Win. Your protégé gets into a position of power? Win. Left or right, everyone wants their wins.

Wins always rubbed me the wrong way. Writing this chapter helped me better understand why. The logic of wins is that you accumulate them on your path to get what you want. Wins are like conquered territories. Battles won. The victories you accumulate in a war. Investors, funders, political parties, and philanthropists who back these organizations and movements place their bets accordingly: if you are good at winning, we back you. It divides the universe into zeros and ones. Nothing else matters.

Writing this, I realized that I got my first lesson in the tactics of getting wins in 2009. Liza had joined us from Chicago as an intern in Barcelona. She had just finished volunteering for the Obama 2008 presidential campaign. I loved listening to her stories about the campaign machinery: canvassing homes, going from door to door. The script was extraordinary. It was stripped down, designed to get wins and nothing else. It went something like this:

1. Knock.
2. Ask if they plan to vote Obama.
3.1 "Yes," take note, make sure they know how to vote, and move on.

3.2   "Not sure," talk to them, ask again, move on.

3.3   "No," don't waste time, move on.

Creating the Right Kind of #Win Society

It was magical, so efficient! You talk only to those who are willing to agree, don't waste a calorie on the others. It's just that I kept thinking about the others. I had never seen anything quite like it. I found the idea so alien, to walk around a neighborhood, *and not talk to everyone.* What kind of community was that? Years later, I saw the same playbook again. This time it was salespeople from successful software companies who taught me how to work through sales leads. Don't waste time with people who don't want to buy now. Move on to the next. Wins, I feared, were creating the very social bubbles that create further division in our communities, by feeding the mind-set that put the quick win over all else. Including what others might lose when you win.

Don't get me wrong, I love the fact that Denisa won the junk food tax and that Katherine won marriage equality and an end to Draconian punishments for abortion. But more important, I loved *how* they won. Denisa is a member of the community she serves. There is no point in collecting wins that don't nurture her community as a whole. After all, she fights to overcome division. Families found out why their children suffered diabetes. Then they connected the dots and saw how their healthy traditions had been lost too. They learned about the lost culture of food that had once united their community. It wasn't just a matter of whether you like to eat junk food but how food with no nutritional value came to be the only option available. No experts brought the idea of putting a tax on junk food to the community. Families developed the idea as a way to restore their health and traditions. For Denisa a win is only good when it builds trust in the community. She would trade trust for wins, any day.

This kind of slowness is a sign of care, of true inclusion, of not being afraid to get involved with humans. And it works.

The Real Win Is Buried in the Human Mess

The human mess. Denisa, Albina, Katherine, Jane, Mark, Yuraima—they all thrive on it. It sparks their social imagination. It fuels their long journeys to change. But for most people in power, this human mess is a pain. Why bother nurturing relationships and communities when you can divide the whole and collect your wins? And division works wonders. It was Richard Nixon, in his presidential campaign, who first invented the idea of using abortion as a divisive idea to drive a wedge between socially conservative Democrats and their party.[14]

It was an invented division. People hadn't cared to let the issue of abortion define their political affiliations until it became a quick fix for Nixon to win power. It worked. And strategists went on to push it to an absurd extreme, continuing to further divide communities in the United States. Following the US Supreme Court's *Dobbs* decision in 2022, some state legislatures like California and Oregon went on to protect abortion rights in their constitutions.[15] Others, like Texas, enacted draconian laws that allow citizens to become abortion vigilantes, institute $100,000 fines, threaten life imprisonment to abortion providers, and open the courts to equate abortion to murder charges with potential death penalties.[16] This continues to further divide communities across the United States. As a result, it now tops the wins list of organizations on all sides of the battle. Only, this quick fix is toxic, like a nuclear bomb, causing irreparable harm to our communities and relationships.

Social Imagination, Our Best Defense

Denisa's work is all about community health. And it improves democracy. Her movement holds leaders accountable, gives women and girls a voice, and feeds brilliant new policy ideas like the junk food tax into the Tribal Council. Relationships build resilience in the community, against attempts to divide people. Denisa is so central because she dives right into the human mess. She knows her community, takes time to listen, and helps out. All this builds trust. Trust opens hearts and minds, allowing Denisa to bring new knowledge to the community. Over time, creative fresh ideas for the future emerge. My good friend David Lubell, a seasoned activist and movement builder, puts it like this: "Community organizing is wonderful. But it becomes magic when, instead of simply insisting on a single issue, it sparks collective creativity." Social imagination, our best defense against divisive power politics.

Bury the Tiger

If Denisa is building the defenses against division, the story of Ireland (told in Chapter 1) shows us how leaders can withstand the temptations of divisive politics in the first place. The Celtic Tiger, Ireland's bet to chase growth at all costs in the 1990s, is central to understanding this story. People hoped that the Fast Lane could outpace their more profound problems. With the 2007–2008 financial crisis, however, the gamble ended in tears of shame, humiliation, and suffering. Grappling with the devastating reality of a broken economy, severe inequality, and abuse by the church, people realized that they had no place to return.

So they opened up to new ideas. After economists had so evidently led the country astray, leaders turned to practitioners from the Slow Lane. People like Katherine Zappone and Jane

Suiter. They wanted to slow things down, listen, and build bridges. It really is an extraordinary turn of events, when you think about it. Katherine was a gay theologian, professor, feminist, social entrepreneur, and minister serving in a conservative cabinet. Unafraid of talking theology, and deeply rooted in activism, she offered a moral compass. She seemed to embody a way forward for Ireland.

Jane and her network of academics, for their part, offered a new tool: the citizen assembly. It wasn't a fix to democracy but an experimental vehicle that would be quick to deploy. It represented the five Slow Lane Principles:

1. It promised to hold the urgency, by letting the assembly take its time to deliberate complex issues.

2. It promised to listen to everyone, selecting people at random from all over Ireland.

3. It promised to share the agency, by letting the assembly develop new proposals.

4. It encouraged curiosity, by guiding members of the assembly through the stages of unlearning, seeking inspiration from experts and activists, and letting new ideas emerge.

5. It used technology as an enabler, not betting on digital forms of participation but as a way to select, convene, and facilitate human dialogue.

It is fair to say that going slow proved the faster way to update the constitution.

The Wins We Want

Wins aren't all bad, and the Slow Lane loves a good win! Done right, such wins allow everyone to experience a better future. Become less afraid of change. Citizen assemblies in Ireland did just that. As did the junk food tax in the Navajo Nation, the prison council in Pentonville Prison, or the seventy municipalities in Peru that contracted recyclers even before the Ley del Reciclador was adopted. These wins were profoundly different in three ways from the canvassing that Liza had described.

First, instead of putting people on the spot to say yes or no, they invited them to become part of creating a new answer, to join the magic as it happened. Second, they considered everyone a member of the community, instead of creating an us-versus-them logic. Third, they never stopped the conversation, knowing that their neighbor would always be there, in the community. And that one day, they too would join.

= 7 =

Your Slow Lane

Part of being awake is slowing down
enough to notice what we say and do.

Pema Chödrön

My wonderful editor Steve Piersanti calls the Slow Lane a fractal concept, meaning that it plays out in similar ways at different scales, from the intimate to the global.

And it is true: we have seen how the Slow Lane can inspire inner work. It helped me unravel my theater of listening. It can inspire us to change the way we relate to our loved ones and our family, as it did when I became more honest and open with my children. The same change can play out in a group or team, unlocking new possibilities. Slow Lane thinking can inspire transformative change in communities, as it did with United for Brownsville, where families are now the experts working alongside social care professionals to change what it means to grow up in the neighborhood. It can make our organizations or movements more impactful, as it did for Germany's Green Party, User Voice, Peru's waste-pickers, or Ireland's human rights campaigners. Governments, both local (like Sefton) and national (like Iceland), can practice the Slow Lane Principles to

---

achieve real change, faster. And the Slow Lane can inspire us to think differently about responding to, or preventing national or even international, crises and divisions like climate change or inequality.

"Fractal" is a beautiful way to capture what I have tried to share with you in writing this book. The Slow Lane doesn't just play out at all these scales but demands that we understand how interconnected they are. I doubt that there can be a good leader in a Slow Lane movement, if they don't tackle their inner Fast Lane thinking too. Dorica's story shows how interconnected these scales can be. Both Dorica and her husband suffer rare diseases, and caring for their daughter Oana, they developed a profound understanding of what it takes to give just a single person access to learning and opportunity. Their curiosity first led them to have Oana diagnosed in Italy, which in turn set them on a path to create a national association that tapped into global knowledge. It went on to show, at all scales, what the future of health care should look like. Dorica continues to operate at all scales, applying the Slow Lane Principles. She is as active in her family as she is in the NoRo care center as she is in national and even international rare disease movements and bodies.

Finding Our Way
to the New (Uncomfortable) Answers

You have read about the Slow Lane Principles. What now? I started this book by saying that the Slow Lane offers new answers, whether for your family life, your work, your business, or your engagement or activism in society.

My personal relationship with the Slow Lane has developed over fifty years of my life. I have written about it not because my life is all that interesting, but because I wanted to share with you how there are many paths into the Slow Lane—epic or small, direct or long-winded. Some of my earliest childhood memories were of the Slow Lane. Not about participating but about how I was brought up with a prejudice against Germany's environmental movement, a prejudice that took me decades to overcome. Later, as a student of architecture, a field trip to Soweto in South Africa inspired me to chart my course into the Slow Lane. It led me to Caracas, where a single day with a young architect, Yuraima Martín, taught me all I ever needed to know about the Slow Lane. It blew up all my preconceptions about what it means to be of service, and what greatness should really look like. A few years later, I co-initiated a Slow Lane movement myself, to flip the zombie of public procurement and put the spending of cities to more meaningful use.

The more I saw of the Slow Lane, the more it began to challenge me. How should I go about my job, how could I reframe my mission, what does success look like? In the end, it was the relationship to my daughters that brought it all home to me. As I tried to be a good father, I realized how hard it was to put trust into action, to liberate myself from the false comfort of the conventions of Fast Lane success. I could not have made sense of this, if I hadn't seen this in action in the least trusting of places: a notorious prison in London. If Kevin Reilly, the prison governor, could trust his inmates enough to ask them for help to make his prison safer, surely I could do the same at home with my daughters.

None of this is easy, not because it is hard to do but because our mind-sets have been framed all our lives. We have been conditioned to trust the simple promise of the Fast Lane: that dominance is more reliable than trusting the people around us.

Your Turn to Play All the Scales

Here are some ways in which you can apply the fractal Slow Lane Principles at different scales—from family to society. I will walk you through each scale, highlighting the most relevant insights for each. The Slow Lane Parent, the Slow Lane Leader, the Slow Lane Volunteer, the Slow Lane Movement, the Slow Lane Business, and the Slow Lane Government.

The Slow Lane Parent

> To stop pretending [in listening], I have to keep returning to find my answer to the two questions that help us reveal our true intentions: (1) How far am I willing to trust others to know what is right? And (2) How superior am I in my vision or ability to make that judgment?

I wrote this in the conclusion of Chapter 2, "Listen." If you believe, rationally, that this is true, do it. I noticed how I had been cheating myself for years, making myself believe that I was listening when really I was being judgmental or passive-aggressive. My teenage daughters, of course, saw right through it and rolled their eyes. At one point I looked at myself, questioning my justifications for being the benevolent dictator in their lives. Seeing this was the first step in a process to face my fears, to get to the bottom of the simple question: Do I really want to empower those around me? And if I do, is there any better way than showing them my unconditional trust?

The insight here is to find the courage and challenge yourself, and ask what your listening reveals about your true intentions. And if these intentions really are what you want them to be.

Talking to my friend Georg revealed the kinds of fears we store up in ourselves, fears that push us to do the opposite of what we believe to be right: the fear of losing our credibility as a protector and losing our power as a leader. He said: "Maybe there was also something else that caused me to react the way I did. I can't quite put my finger on it. I think I felt a bit overwhelmed, put on the spot. Vulnerable. It was a terrible feeling.

I may have felt that I don't have any real answers to the threat climate change poses to our children. But at the same time, as a father, I am supposed to protect them, know all the answers."

The insight here is that we should not be afraid to acknowledge these fears. Pretending to be in control when we aren't will tear us, and our relationships, apart. Instead, the Slow Lane shows us how to be upfront about these uncertainties, extend more trust, and share the agency with our children, to become a part of our new answers. The Slow Lane Parent does this, knowing that it will lead to more truthful relationships and better answers. It is also an investment in the self-efficacy of our children, their belief, and confidence in that they too can achieve real change.

The takeaway for parents is to not be afraid of what you might discover about yourself, your fears, and how you use your powers. Instead of focusing on problems, use the Slow Lane Principles as a way to build healthier, more genuine relationships with your children.

The Slow Lane Leader

What holds true for our relationships at home holds true for our professional behavior too. I found myself living through the same challenges in my professional life, until I challenged myself to ask what success looks like. I realized, painfully, that I put a ton of value on being seen as the smartest person in every room. Success for me wasn't about money but being right. I justified this with my pursuit of a good and an important social mission. All this proved unsustainable as a way of organizing change, and it was unsustainable for me as a person. It reminds me of Albina Ruiz realizing that her movement would stagnate for as long as she didn't allow everyone to lead and create their own solutions. This inflection point forced me to look for new ways, to correct course. Like Albina and many others, I found the answer in letting go and opening up, to support others to contribute and take charge.

Whether you are a leader in business, government, a non-profit, or a community organization, the journey to meaningful change will lead through the Slow Lane Principles. Time and again, the traditional forms of leadership by executive decision have delivered mostly ineffective quick fixes. When public leaders rushed to action following the 2007–2008 financial crisis, for instance, they chose not to involve the people they serve, instead trusting in experts. The result: even fifteen years later, tens of millions remain impoverished and unemployed. Business leaders do just the same, in their quest for speed to succeed in the Fast Lane. They want to avoid doing harm, but in their race to the top they cut corners. They avoid anything that slows them down. Much of our public narrative celebrates this style of decisive leadership and the disruption it creates. But with every problem this kind of leadership solves, it creates another, deepening the divides in our communities.

The insight here is to embrace the truth that slowing down will get you there faster. Internalize the fact that quick fixes will cause more harm than good. For me, that meant a reckoning with my ego. Did I really believe that success was about me coming out looking smart, imposing my solution? Eventually I realized that I had much more fun solving with others, stepping into enabling roles myself. This is consistent with what everyone from Albina Ruiz to Dr. Sanjeev Aurora described. They feel immense joy in the work of empowering others to lead. Whatever the chemistry we release when solving not *for* but *with*, it works. As you invite others to contribute and lead with their ideas, you will begin to unlock the magic of creativity and imagination.

The second, related insight is to remember that reframing is a new skill to be learned in the Slow Lane. Reframing allows you to look for new angles to find a radically different *question* to start with. Dorica took her daughter's disease of one to build a movement for a million rare disease patients by focusing on what they all had in common: an experience of never fitting into any system. The stories I have shared in this book reframed the role of people who suffered from being passive subjects in need to seeing them for their capacity to contribute. In other words, the stories reframed problems into assets, which in turn unlocked everything else.

If all this seems hard to do, it is! Our brains (and the brains of those around us) are wired to want just the opposite: quick, heroic results. But the magic of the Slow Lane is unleashed when you dare to think slow. That is inconvenient at first, but behind that initial temptation lies the opportunity to collectively discover transformative new answers.

The Slow Lane Volunteer

Chances are that you are volunteering already: 862 million people do so, every year, giving the equivalent of 61 million full-time employees.[1] That's more than twice as many people as all the armies in the world put together. How can you apply the Slow Lane Principles in your volunteering practice?

A good starting point is to think about how the Slow Lane can make your contribution more valuable. It could help you become more discerning about where and how you volunteer. The Slow Lane is all about listening and sharing the ability to solve, with the goal of empowering those who are suffering to become contributors. Volunteering work can lack that aspect of empowerment, focusing more on serving a problem instead of solving it. An example of that would be how Rosanne Haggerty started her work, serving in a homeless shelter as a young graduate. She realized that the work she was doing wasn't actually helping people. Instead, she was helping the shelter run the shelter.

Her insight came from listening to the people experiencing homelessness, who kept asking for help finding a job or a home. Following this insight, Rosanne changed course and invested time in helping where she actually solved homelessness. She went on to solve homelessness in fourteen cities.

Here is the first insight. Being discerning can mean that you choose carefully where you contribute, to find where you can help bring about real change. Or it could be even more transformative, if you apply the Slow Lane Principles to improve what is already happening around you. If, for example, you work in a shelter that doesn't really solve a problem for the homeless, you could start to involve others, to help them find a job or a home. At Ashoka we call this the "teams of teams" approach. You get more done by combining different groups to truly make a difference. And this, by the way, was precisely how Rosanne brought many important support services into the Prince George Hotel. I am sharing Rosanne's story here not to put you under pressure to become a systems-changing social entrepreneur like her. Naturally, that would be great. Denisa Livingston told me what many others said: She doesn't judge people by how much or how they volunteer. She welcomes everyone to their abilities and makes sure there are many fulfilling ways to contribute to build a healthier Navajo Nation. I would love for you to experience your volunteering in this way.

The second insight is this: over time, who knows what can happen. Remember, this is the Slow Lane, after all! The takeaway for volunteers is to use the Slow Lane Principles to gently challenge how you contribute and how things are done around you. Explore your comfort zone as you discern what works, and what could be different, to find your role.

The Slow Lane Movement

I have used the term "movement" generously in this book. At first, I was tempted to refer to them as "communities" instead.

In some cases, there is a strong collective identity around what people are doing, as is the case with Denisa's Diné Health Alliance or the German environmental movement. In other instances, participants barely know that they are part of a movement for change, like the learners who participate in a Project ECHO training. Identity can be a powerful tool to build a collective sense of belonging, as was the case with the waste-pickers in Peru who reinvented themselves as recyclers. When I refer to "movements," I simply want to capture all those who are involved.

The stories in this book offer countless insights as to how you can apply the Slow Lane Principles in practice, depending on your purpose. They may also encourage you to further de-velop your movement's ability to listen, share the agency, and nurture your curiosity in creative new ways. Leaders of Karuna and GLS Bank in Germany, for example, realized that their respective movements of young activists were mostly discon-nected. In 2021 they created Goldener Raum (Golden Space), a meeting that brought together young activists from privileged backgrounds, many of whom were active in Fridays for Future, and young activists who had experienced homelessness.[2] The encounter celebrated challenging questions such as how a cli-mate strike might relate to the challenges of extreme poverty or domestic abuse. Together, the young activists created new common ground. Both groups came out stronger.

The first insight for movements is that social change rarely happens in less than forty years. It often takes generations. Few movements are upfront about the long journey ahead of them, treating every week like an urgent battle to be won right away. The result: stagnation, frustration, or burnout. In desper-ation, movements may then opt for divisive tactics that promise quick wins over the (seemingly) slower practices of inclusion. Successful Slow Lane movements adapt their strategies to be-come more sustainable and inclusive for the long haul. Or lie in wait for their window of opportunity to achieve big change peacefully, as the gay and abortion rights movements did in Ireland. Albina's story is a textbook example of a movement that always, and intentionally, avoided divisive actions to lay the ground for the alliances that would unlock the next achievements on their path.

The second insight is that movements should think hard about how they can be of service. In the stories told throughout this book, movements succeeded in winning the long game by being of service. Yuraima, her father César, Father Joseito, and Doris Barrento have been fixtures in Catuche, the slum in Caracas, for more than three decades. Every day they support the community on their path to self-determination. That matters in a country that has been in political turmoil and economic freefall for decades already and has helped the community overcome many setbacks—from floods to gang wars. Dorica is not just focusing on changing national policy, but her movement is an essential service provider to people suffering from rare diseases. Being of service is so strategic because it helps empower victims of injustice or those for whom change may be hardest to become part of creating solutions.

Doing this builds invaluable trust and helps challenge preconceptions of what a community for change looks like. Remember, in Peru, waste-pickers ended up working side by side with business and government leaders to change everything. That could only happen because the movement was in some way of service to everyone. Finally, being of service is key to the practice of social imagination. By doing and working together, immersed in finding better ways to do what needs to be done, the kind of collective ideas begin to emerge that can lead to real change. In successful Slow Lane movements, being of service is what makes everything else possible.

The takeaway for movements is that they have to embrace

the fact that change is slow. Knowing where you are on your journey is key to your success. Feeding on urgency alone will lead to frustration and divisive action. Instead, focus on being of service to build community and lower the barrier to participation. This in turn will unlock your ability to deliver the real change, faster.

The Slow Lane Business

Millions of people start businesses to better the world. According to the 2020–21 *Global Entrepreneurship Monitor Report*, more than 71.2 percent of entrepreneurs in the United States stated that their motivation to start a business was "to make a difference in the world." In the UK that percentage was 53 percent, in Germany 39.4 percent, in Brazil it was 75.7 percent, and in South Africa 81.4 percent. The Slow Lane shows ways in which entrepreneurs can turn their desire into a reality.[3]

The first insight is that entrepreneurs who want to make a difference can use the Slow Lane Principles to test their decisions and harmonize their desire for profit and wealth with their hope to do good. Like the protagonists of our stories, they too will face challenges and moments of truth. Am I going to pursue fast growth or dominance in my market at the cost of sowing division in my community or society? Am I in the business of selling quick fixes, or am I contributing to meaningful change?

The second insight is about how to use the connected nature of all business to achieve real change. Most entrepreneurs start their business to gain independence. But they rarely operate in isolation. The Slow Lane challenges you to go a step further, asking you to extend your independence to others by applying the Slow Lane Principles. For this, you will need to not just change the way you work; you'll need to build bridges and put your investors, clients, partners, and employees on the kind of journey of discovery that lets you cocreate your shared vision for change. What worked for Albina to align the vision of waste-pickers, industrialists, and politicians in Peru can be applied to entrepreneurs as well. That's why Ashoka calls people like Albina, Rosanne, Denisa, Simon, and Sanjeev *social entrepreneurs*. Their goal may not be profit, but their behavior is entrepreneurial as they envision change and help rearrange the world around them.

The third insight is to stay alert for the practices that undermine real change. Think of them as quick fixes that look promising and effective only on first sight. Businesses that practice listening to manipulate their customers are doing little to empower them; building technology around your desire to maximize profits may incentivize divisive social behaviors; offering an engineering fix to a problem like waste management may overlook the important human dynamics; or insisting on the "all in" formula for startups that have good reason to blend digital and human services. Knowing what bad looks like is just as important as knowing what the new good should look like.

The fourth insight is that even if the transition from Fast Lane to Slow Lane cannot happen overnight, the underlying moral compass needs to be sharp from day one. The Slow Lane has shown creative and sophisticated ways to make real change happen in incredibly complex circumstances. At any point of these journeys they demonstrated an almost perfect clarity of vision. And they accepted the discomfort of maintaining a high degree of flexibility to respond to change not by compromising standards but by lifting them. In short, entrepreneurs and leaders in business have to learn that if something has to give, it shouldn't be the principles. Resilience in your business will mean that you are capable of finding creative ways to hold the tension of staying true to your values and principles at all times, even if real change has yet to materialize.

The takeaway for entrepreneurs and business leaders
here is simple. Don't stop holding yourself accountable to the
principles, and don't go this journey alone. All businesses are
connected, and the biggest impact you can have is to take your
clients, partners, investors, and employees along. Together
you will be able to unlock a whole new level of creativity and
imagination.

The Slow Lane Government

I see the role of public servants, and the government more
broadly, as integral to the Slow Lane. If that is you, I hope that
you find value in these stories. The Slow Lane offers a variety
of insights for governments and public servants. In the story
about Sefton in Chapter 2, I wrote: "Frustration turned into
a mission: Sefton's leaders invested themselves in making the
best of a situation they could not control. They became a listening government."

The first insight here is that there is a path for government
to embrace the Slow Lane Principles and become a listening
government that empowers people. In Sefton it wasn't just a set
of principles but the deep personal engagement of local leaders
and public servants. Their journey provides valuable insights
to public servants anywhere.

This brings us to the second insight for governments. If you
experience inexplicable setbacks, you may well have encountered a zombie. As I explain in Chapter 4, "zombie systems" are
bureaucracies that work against not just the public interest but
even the interests of government leaders. I have shown how we
can uncover the intricate root causes, like public procurement,
that cause dysfunction across many critical public services
and infrastructure. When public servants and other Slow Lane
movements work together, they can flip these zombies, turning
great pain into a potentially delightful force for good. People

in government should be alert to dig up and reveal these zombies, because of the widespread disruption they cause to social change—in government and beyond. I hope my story about procurement delight helps you imagine ways in which such projects generate excitement. To achieve that, don't be afraid to create an environment where imposters are welcome.

The third insight is about the dangers of Fast Lane leadership. This book is intentionally framed against the background of politicians' rushed response to the 2007–2008 financial crisis. We can learn a lot from the political mishaps, not only in the immediate response to the financial crisis (see "The Slow Lane Leader" discussion, above) but also in the divisive politics that followed years later. It was the poor handling of the financial crisis that laid the ground for divisive politics, like nationalism in Catalonia, Brexit, and the Trump presidency. Ireland stands out for finding a path out of this divisive climate, by turning the rough hand history had dealt it into an opportunity to rebuild its democracy. Going slow proved a much faster way to reform the constitution. Just as it proved a faster way to recover Iceland's economy.

I concluded Chapter 6, "Heal Democracy," with a call to action that should resonate with public servants in particular: *focus on wins that guarantee everyone a better future, instead of racking up short-term victories that only deepen divides.*

The takeaway for governments and public servants here is simple. Don't shy away from engaging with the messiness of human relationships, especially when your impulse tells you to rush into action. The right answer is always to get involved with people, the better if you can spark their creativity.

Change Is Hard and Slow. Enjoy It!

Real change is hard. But the Slow Lane promises to get you there faster! The point I'm trying to make is that the Slow Lane isn't fast, but it is faster than all else. The Fast Lane represents false hope, a mirage, that won't take you to the right place. From parenting to leading in government, applying the Slow Lane Principles demands a close look in the mirror, and at least a small reckoning with our Fast Lane mind-sets and ways. That's why it is so important, as you embark on your journey to slow down and achieve real change, to be compassionate with yourself and those around you. You did not create the Fast Lane, after all.

Real change will take a long time. Knowing this is essential to succeed because it helps you see through the tempting promises of quick fixes. There is no quick fix. But just because the journey is long doesn't mean that you should not adopt the Slow Lane Principles with urgency. Depending on your context, that may be hard or very hard to do. Even if adopting the principles cannot happen overnight, you should be uncompromisingly clear and upfront about the Fast Lane ways for as long as they persist. As you begin to make uncomfortable changes, take comfort from knowing that the Slow Lane will make you, and everyone else, feel better. Not because you are part of a morally superior cause, but because the Slow Lane works like the relationships we like best: it is about practicing community and care with the added bonus that together you will be able to imagine truly transformative change. Use joy as your north star: if applying the Slow Lane Principles begins to feel like a battle, you will probably have to dial things down a bit and go back to holding the urgency.

Conclusion

Where and How to Start

The most important resource for caring is time.

Joan C. Tronto

You have read *The Slow Lane*. Now what? If you are interested in getting started, I propose that you focus on the first two Slow Lane Principles. Hold your urgency and listen. These two principles will lead you to all else. Here is why. Unless you hold the urgency, you cannot practice listening or anything else that matters in the Slow Lane. Don't get caught up in chasing wins at all costs, as they will only feed division. And don't give into the tyranny of urgency. It will kill all the good things, as you rush into action. And unless you listen, free from theater and pretending, you cannot share the agency and empower others. Or practice meaningful curiosity. When you hold the urgency and listen, the path to the other principles will unfold.

#1 Hold the Urgency

Holding the urgency forces you to stare down your Fast Lane instinct to jump into action, to find quick answers when there are none. It can be very counterintuitive. Because it is so hard to do at moments of crisis, and when the stakes are high, it is so important to get started now to practice this new skill. Remember, holding the urgency is not about being complacent or not caring. Quite the opposite: it is knowing that when everything tells you to rush to action—when your passion is burning high, when the stakes are at their highest, and when everyone tells you that there is no alternative—it is time for you to slow things down, to engage yourself in the complexity of human relationships, and find that alternative. These moments of crisis can take different forms. They may take the form of a real, identifiable crisis, like the financial crisis of 2007–2008. They may play out subconsciously, a fear burning inside you. Like worrying about your reputation or about the future well-being of your children.

I found it necessary to truly internalize and trust the fact that not rushing to action will get me to the right place faster. Having this clear in my head, and heart, helped me develop alternatives to Fast Lane behaviors. The Slow Lane has shown us how to hold the urgency in a variety of situations. At home, in a prison, in a slum, on a waste-heap, during a national crisis, or in a tribal nation. It always starts with confronting our fears. We may be afraid for our children, our planet, our livelihoods, our revenue, our sustainability, our ego, our credibility, our power, what unites us, or our reputation.

Holding the urgency may or may not actually slow things down. But it is about holding the tension between our fears and knowing how important it is to empower others if we are to succeed. In my home not much has changed about the actual question I ask on Saturdays, but my daughters would say it is all different now. That's because our power dynamics have changed. They see the question no longer as a threat but an open invitation. Similarly, things haven't significantly slowed down at Pentonville Prison, but prisoners are invited to become part of the decisions that directly affect their safety, well-being, and journey back into society. The real change is in how much Kevin Reilly, the governor, values the contribution of the prisoners.

#2 Listen

Which brings us to listening. Once you learn to withstand the temptation of taking control and rushing to action, real listening can follow. The Slow Lane prompted me to dig deeper into the central question of this book: How much do we want to trust others in their ability to self-determine and make a valuable contribution? Or asked differently: How much better do we think we are? Knowing the answer will help us become intentional, stop pretending, and start listening for real.

In Chapter 2, "Listen," I wrote that there is only so much pretending we can do. It is only when your mind-set shifts to wanting to extend real trust and engagement that you can stop pretending. How you turn this into action will require some experimentation. I found it helpful to open up to my daughters about what I want to change in how I relate to them. This allowed them to provide feedback and signal when I risked falling into old patterns or creating a *1984* moment, as they called it. Pentonville Prison needed the help of User Voice to practice genuine listening, as there simply was no way that prisoners would feel safe in opening up to prison and probation officials. In Brownsville it took years of community organizing to build a trusted foundation, free from systemic racism, to do the actual listening. And in Sefton as well as in the Irish citizen assemblies, governments found creative new ways to become true listeners not just by sharing power but by seeing citizens for their abilities to contribute.

In this diversity of practices lies the clue on how to get things right. There is no one way to truly listen, to become a listening person, business, community organization, movement, or government. Instead, listening has to be bespoke to those who want to be heard. For some groups that is easy to organize. People with privilege tend to respond more easily to an invitation. For others, such an invitation will be nothing but pretense. This is where you should focus your energy, not as an afterthought but as your core purpose. This is why holding the urgency makes space for listening and is the right place to start. The more you do it, the more it will change the way you do almost everything, as you let go of your Fast Lane ways.

Now Hold the Urgency, to Let All Flavors of Listening Bloom

To help you get started, I share some ideas as to how you can apply these first two Slow Lane Principles at different scales, from parenting to government. They all start with a question to help reframe your outlook and set you on a new path.

Start as a Parent

Ask yourself, what am I afraid of when I pretend to listen, or impose my answers on my child? And then ask yourself, do you want your child to grow their sense of self-efficacy, their belief that they can make a difference?

From here, you can be more intentional and practice how to turn your impulse to rush to action into the practice of holding your urgency to listen. A good sign that things are moving in the right direction is if you are getting honest feedback, good or bad, about how you are doing. This too needs practice as your child learns how to put feelings into words, and how safe it is to be open with you.

Start as a Leader

Ask yourself if you really believe that you have to be a hero who knows best, one who carries the burden of big decisions on behalf of others. How can the way you listen become a way for you to achieve better results, and let those around you *experience* that they are an important part of the choices you make?

From here, practice new behaviors with those around you. You can, for example, challenge yourself to involve those around you in deliberations that you would have resolved alone. I found it useful to practice being vulnerable in front of others by speaking up about my fears or uncertainties. Seeing how this did not cause any harm has let me open up and include others, even when the stakes are high. It also created an environment in which others feel safer to share their true feelings and opinions.

Start as a Volunteer

What does how you are being of service tell you about how you're listening? Are you treating people as problems to be cared for, or can they contribute according to their full abilities?

From here, you can expand the possibilities to let others contribute. You may well have to slow down a bit to make that happen, and do something new, to let the person make their contribution. Use your interactions to listen for what others really need, and what they can offer. Show that you believe in their ability to contribute to make a difference and that you are there to stay.

Start as a Movement

Challenge your listening by looking at how your movement listens at times of crisis. Have you found a way to remain open to new voices and ideas from unexpected places? Or are you responding by placing the leadership in the hands of a few and taking a harder, maybe more divisive line?

From here, you can build the structures, capabilities, and

behaviors that make it easy (and safe) for your movement to hold the urgency and promote great listening at all times. Done right, you will see more diversity in leadership and opinion.

Start as a Business

Are you great listeners? Chances are that you are better at holding your urgency and listening when times are good, less so when you're in a pickle. Where can you begin to change this behavior and start listening better so that you can always be on course to contribute to positive change?

From here, practice new behaviors and look out for the pain points where urgency undermines your purpose—like mindsets, business fundamentals, products, services, partnerships, skills, and capabilities. Over time, confidence should grow that at times of crisis, answers can be found by engaging in relationships, and not by autocratic leadership, whatever that means in your business. Depending on how far you are willing to take this, you can study new organizational models like "everyone leads" and shared ownership structures that can best enable shared responsibility.

Start as a Government

Look for the situations in which your government typically stops the listening and rushes to action. How can you develop a new behavior at times of crisis and go out to listen?

From here, start by challenging the prevailing expectation that citizens are passive users of services, defined by their needs. Develop your ability to hold the urgency and your new listening practice by focusing on a hard-to-reach group of people. This effort should be designed to unfold naturally, at the speed of trust, instead of fixed timeframes. Let this group push you to develop a new approach that works for them. Government leaders, for their part, should start by internalizing the Slow

Lane form of leadership that intuitively engages people, instead of shutting them out, at moments of crisis.

From Here, Your Path Will Unfold

Getting started will let you find truthful answers to questions about your identity, your purpose, and how far you are willing to go in trusting others. These three questions apply to you as a parent as much as to a government.

I encourage you to not worry about much more as you get started. When you hold the urgency and listen, you're not going to know what will happen. You will step into the unknown. And that can be uncomfortable. But it is a risk worth taking because once you do that, the path will unfold.

As you weigh your courage to hold the urgency against the risks of the unknown, remind yourself that holding the urgency is the best way of *reducing* risk. The risk of losing our democracy, the risk of more division, the risk of feeding the always problems, the risk of not empowering our children, the risk of not caring. Whatever brought you here, the Slow Lane offers to take you to the right place.

Putting the Slow Lane Principles into practice, you will rebuild your role in the world. Holding the urgency and listening is a risk worth taking. Because it is only from here that a new vision and your path to change can emerge.

The Slow Lane
Discussion Guide

I hope that reading *The Slow Lane* provided you with some new insights about how the Fast Lane mind-set undermines our goal to contribute to real change. The book presents strategies and practices as to how you can put the Slow Lane Principles to use—whether individually, as part of a team or group, as an organization, or as an ecosystem. By "ecosystem," I mean seeing your organization as part of a dynamic system that includes other stakeholders, such as your partners, clients, customers, supply chain, regulators, policy makers, people whose lives are affected by what you do. Many stories in the book show how the Slow Lane can help such systems change.

I have organized the discussion prompts here to be considered at the personal level, at the team or group level, and at the organization and ecosystem level.

Questions for yourself:

1. Where are the Fast Lane mind-sets and behaviors in your life? Having identified them, try to see them in a new light and see if they really provide the safety and promise you wish for.

2. In honesty, how much do you trust others to be fully capable to make valuable contributions? And if you do, are you intentional in putting this into practice through listening and sharing the agency?

3. How do you react in moments of crisis? What are your weak spots in which you rush to action and resort to more autocratic behaviors? What Fast Lane fears and mind-sets can you uncover in this reflection?

4. Can you identify a couple of relationships and situations in which you can practice holding your urgency, listening, and sharing the agency?

Questions for your team / group:

1. What is our mode of responding to crisis? Do we rush into action, or do we hold our urgency?

2. Can we agree on a situation where rushing to action, opting for a quick fix, did more harm than good?

3. Let's acknowledge that we often pretend to listen, intentionally or unwittingly. How does it feel to come to terms with that as a team / group, and what actions come to mind to do something about it?

4. What regular practices can we create in our team / group to cultivate the Slow Lane Principles?

Questions for your organization:

1. What elements of our organizational model, our business model, our products / services, and the way we work adhere to Fast Lane Principles? In what ways are we contributing to divides instead of making progress on the "always" problems?

2. Where can we start to use the Slow Lane Principles to uncover opportunities to improve our practices and behaviors?

3. What mind-sets and incentives prevail in our organizations that lead to Fast Lane behaviors, and how can we start to incentivize Slow Lane mind-sets and practices?

4. How can we create pathways for everyone to become a real contributor in our organization?

Questions for your ecosystem:

1. What are the "always" problems that we should be tackling, to transform the system?

2. How can we reframe our goals, so that they both tackle the "always" problems and lead us to solve *with* rather than *for* people?

3. Are we locked into a single solution, and do we risk imposing it on others? How can we nurture our curiosity to promote a more flexible approach to change?

4. Do we have pathways in place for anyone to join our movement or ecosystem and contribute, or do we demand that people submit to our mind-sets and ideas?

Notes

FOREWORD

1. Karen Bannan and Hana Schank, eds., "The Commons," Public Interest Technology at New America, https://wearecommons.us/ (accessed December 20, 2022).

2. Sascha Haselmayer, "Fast Tech, Slow Change," *The Commons*, The Slow Lane Issue (online), January 28, 2021, https://wearecommons.us/fast -tech-slow-change/ (accessed December 20, 2022).

3. Carlo Rovelli, "The Big Idea: Why Relationships Are the Key to Existence," *The Guardian*, September 5, 2022, https://www.theguardian.com /books/2022/sep/05/the-big-idea-why-relationships-are-the-key-to-existence (accessed December 21, 2022).

INTRODUCTION

Epigraph: Lao Tzu, *Tao Te Ching*, sixth century BC.

1. Karla Adam, "Occupy Wall Street Protests Go Global," *Washington Post*, October 15, 2011.

2. Mark Blyth, *Austerity: The History of a Dangerous Idea* (New York: Oxford University Press, 2013).

3. BBC News, "Iceland Leader Vetoes Bank Repayments Bill," *BBC News*, January 5, 2010, http://news.bbc.co.uk/1/hi/business/8441312.stm (accessed November 20, 2022).

4. American Psychiatric Association, *Diagnostic and Statistical Manual of Mental Disorders*, 1952 (DSM-I 1st edition) and 1968 (DSM-II 2nd edition).

5. Erik Eckholm, "The Same-Sex Couple Who Got a Marriage License in 1971," *New York Times*, May 16, 2015.

6. Cittaslow is an association of 287 cities started in 1999 that self-define as "cities where living is good," expanding the Slow Food philosophy to communities; see https://cittaslow.org/ (accessed January 8, 2023).

7. Daniel Kahneman, *Thinking, Fast and Slow* (New York: Farrar, Straus and Giroux, 2011).

CHAPTER 1

Epigraph: Bill McKibben, Jill Lapore (host), "Episode 4: The Tree Branch," *The Last Archive* (podcast), November 10, 2022.

1. "AKW Brokdorf: Demonstrationen und Gewalt," *PANORAMA*, NDR, November 15, 1976, https://daserste.ndr.de/panorama/archiv/1976/ -,panorama12410.html (accessed November 22, 2022).

2. Walter Giger, "The Rhine Red, the Fish Dead—The 1986 Schweizerhalle Disaster, a Retrospect and Long-Term Impact Assessment," *Environmental Science and Pollution Research* 16, no. 1 (2009): 98–111.

3. Jason Hickel, "Engineering the Township Home: Domestic Transformations and Urban Revolutionary Consciousness," in *Ekhaya: The Politics of Home in KwaZulu-Natal* (Durban: University of KwaZulu-Natal, 2014), 148–53.

4. Oliver Balch, "Radioactive City: How Johannesburg's Townships Are Paying for Its Mining Past," *The Guardian*, July 6, 2015, https://www .theguardian.com/cities/2015/jul/06/radioactive-city-how-johannesburgs -townships-are-paying-for-its-mining-past (accessed November 20, 2022).

5. Kerstine Appunn, "The History Behind Germany's Nuclear Phase-Out," *Clean Energy Wire*, March 9, 2021, https://www.cleanenergywire.org/fact sheets/history-behind-germanys-nuclear-phase-out (accessed November 6, 2022).

6. Barry Commoner, "Can We Survive?," *Washington Monthly* (December 1969): 21.

7. Karrin Hanshew, "The German Autumn, 1977," in *Terror and Democracy in West Germany* (Cambridge: Cambridge University Press, 2012), 192–235.

8. Climate Watch, "Climate Watch Data: Climate Watch. GHG Emissions," World Resources Institute, 2022, https://www.climatewatchdata.org/ghg -emissions (accessed November 6, 2022).

9. Małgorzata Myśliwiec and Krzysztof Stachowicz, "Corruption in Spain and Catalonia after 2008," *Review of Nationalities* 8 (2018): 225–36.

10. Editorial "Quién roba a Cataluña," *El Pais*, March 10, 2017, https:// elpais.com/elpais/2017/03/09/opinion/1489081336_061645.html (accessed November 6, 2022).

11. Pilar Rahola, "Artur Mas: 'Pienso más en las próximas generaciones que en las próximas elecciones,'" *La Vanguardia*, February 24, 2012, https:// www.lavanguardia.com/magazine/20120224/54258645650/artur-mas-generalitat -psoe-pp-cataluna.html (accessed November 6, 2022).

12. Human Rights Committee, "Views adopted by the Committee under article 5 (4) of the Optional Protocol, concerning communication No. 2425/2014," International Covenant on Human Rights, United Nations, March 17, 2017.

13. David M. Farrell and Jane Suiter, *Reimagining Democracy* (Ithaca, NY: Cornell University Press, 2019).

14. Min Reuchamps and Jane Suiter, eds., *Constitutional Deliberative Democracy in Europe* (Colchester: ECPR Press, 2016), 34–52.

15. "How the Story of Abuse in Catholic Church Institutions Emerged," *Irish Times*, November 26, 2009, https://www.irishtimes.com/news/how-the -story-of-abuse-emerged-1.849771 (accessed November 20, 2022).

16. Georg is a made-up name, as my friend asked me not to reveal his real identity.

17. The Foundation for Young Australians, *Missing Young People in Australian News Media* (The Foundation for Young Australians, 2020). T. Notley, M. Dezuanni, H. F. Zhong, and C. Chambers, *News and Young Australians in 2020: How Young People Access, Perceive and Are Affected by News Media, Research Report* (Sydney: Western Sydney University and Queensland University of Technology, 2020).

CHAPTER 2

Epigraph: Gal Beckerman, *The Quiet Before: On the Unexpected Origins of Radical Ideas* (New York: Crown, 2022), 321.

1. Mark Johnson, *Wasted* (New York: Pegasus Books, 2008).

2. Monica Barry, Elizabeth Weaver, Mark Liddle, Bethany Schmidt, Shadd Maruna, Rosie Meek, and Judy Renshaw, "Evaluation of the User Voice Prison and Community Councils: Final Report," University of Strathclyde, University of Cambridge, 2016, https://strathprints.strath.ac.uk /65046/ (accessed November 6, 2022).

3. User Voice, "The Impact of Giving People on Probation a Voice— Transforming Rehabilitation 2015–2021," https://www.uservoice.org/wp -content/uploads/2021/06/Transforming_Rehabilitation_v4.pdf (accessed November 6, 2022).

4. C. Otto Scharmer, *Theory U: Learning from the Future as It Emerges* (Oakland, CA: Berrett-Koehler, 2009).

5. Margaret Thatcher, UK Prime Minister, House of Commons, October 30, 1990.

6. Sally Gainsbury, Jim Pickard, and Andrew Bounds, "Tories Debated Letting Liverpool 'Decline,'" *Financial Times*, December 30, 2011, https://www .ft.com/content/cd6851e2-2d8a-11e1-b5bf-00144feabdco (accessed November 6, 2022).

7. Government of the UK, "Prime Minister's Speech on the Economy," June 7, 2010, London, https://www.gov.uk/government/speeches/prime -ministers-speech-on-the-economy (accessed November 6, 2022).

8. Sascha Haselmayer, "Santa Monica's Austerity Plan Is Turning the City Away from the Future," *Medium*, June 16, 2020, https://medium.com /embracing-austerity/santa-monicas-austerity-plan-is-turning-the-city-away -from-the-future-e2f8381b6e17 (accessed July 19, 2022).

9. John P. Kretzmann and John L. McKnight, *Building Communities from the Inside Out* (Chicago: ACTA Publications, 1993).

CHAPTER 3

Epigraph: Wikipedia's entry for the term "hero" (accessed October 22, 2022).

1. Melissa Haendel et al., "How Many Rare Diseases Are There?," *Nature Reviews Drug Discovery* 19, no. 2 (November 5, 2019).

2. Interview with Edilberto Delgado by the NGO OLAC, "Webinar 1: La vulnerabilidad como punto de convergencia entre la crisis climática y la crisis sanitaria: Aprendiendo de la adversidad," August 11, 2020, https://fb.watch /f2_Lo_-9kP/ (accessed August 22, 2022).

3. Government of Peru, *Decreto Supremo N° 005-2010-MINAM— Reglamento de la Ley N° 29419. Ley que regula la actividad de los recicladores* (Lima: 2010).

4. Community Solutions, "Built for Zero," https://community.solutions /built-for-zero/ (accessed November 2, 2022).

5. New York City Department of Housing Preservation and Development, "The Brownsville Plan," 2017, https://www1.nyc.gov/site/hpd/services-and -information/brownsville.page (accessed July 24, 2022).

6. Mark Winston Griffith and Max Freedman (hosts), "Episode 3: Third Strike," *NPR School Colors* (podcast), October 4, 2019, https://schoolcolors .simplecast.com/episodes/episode-3-third-strike (accessed November 13, 2022). Maurice R. Berube and Marilyn Gittell, *Confrontation at Ocean Hill-Brownsville: The New York School Strikes of 1968* (Westport, CT: Praeger, 1969).

7. United for Brownsville, "We're Making EI Work More Equitably," https://unitedforbrownsville.org/early-intervention-equity/ (accessed November 20, 2022).

CHAPTER 4

Epigraphs: Abraham Kaplan, "The Age of the Symbol—A Philosophy of Library Education," *Library Quarterly* 34, no. 4, (October 1964), 303. Abraham Maslov, *The Psychology of Science* (New York: Harper & Row, 1966).

1. Amyas Morse, "Transforming Rehabilitation: Progress Review," National Audit Office, London, 2019.

2. Macrotrends, "U.K. Crime Rate & Statistics 1990–2022," https://www .macrotrends.net/countries/GBR/united-kingdom/crime-rate-statistics (accessed November 6, 2022).

3. Sabrina L. Miller, "Daley Pushes for Hiring of Disabled," *Chicago Tribune,* July 16, 2003.

4. Department of Justice, "Justice Department Moves to Intervene in Disability Discrimination Suit Against City of Chicago Regarding Pedestrians with Visual Disabilities," April 8, 2021, Washington, DC, https://www.justice.gov/opa/pr/justice-department-moves-intervene-disability-discrimination-suit-against-city-chicago (accessed November 6, 2022).

5. Sascha Haselmayer, "Serving the Citizens, Not the Bureaucracy," Chicago Council on Global Affairs, 2021.

6. Sophie Hardach, "The School That Created a City for the Blind," *BBC Future*, September 20, 2021, https://www.bbc.com/future/article/20210916-the-school-that-change-a-city-into-a-place-for-the-blind (accessed November 6, 2022).

7. Sarah Holder, "In San Diego, 'Smart' Streetlights Spark Surveillance Reform," *Bloomberg CityLab*, August 6, 2020, https://www.bloomberg.com/news/articles/2020-08-06/a-surveillance-standoff-over-smart-streetlights (accessed July 20, 2022).

8. Sascha Haselmayer, "Barcelona's Communications Magic in Public Procurement to Engage the World, and 2% of Residents," Citymart Procurement Institute, March 26, 2020, https://medium.com/citymartinsights/barcelonas-communications-magic-in-public-procurement-to-engage-the-world-and-2-of-residents-71c3c493d944 (accessed July 20, 2022).

9. Barcelona Drets Socials, "Vincles BCN," May 29, 2017, https://youtu.be/NloxhZxZfgQ (accessed July 20, 2022).

10. Helen MacKenzie, "How We Put Our Rural Community in the Driver's Seat for Public Transport Procurement," Citymart Procurement Institute, June 16, 2020, https://medium.com/citymartinsights/rural-public-transport-procurement-putting-communities-firmly-in-the-driving-seat-d090150ae09d?source=friends_link&sk=2119a1320e536d8608679b94439f6858 (accessed July 20, 2022).

CHAPTER 5

Epigraph: Eric Dawson, Sonya Passi, Sascha Haselmayer, Karen Bannan (host), *The Commons Live!* presents "Taking the Slow Lane: Why Technology Isn't the Only Answer," New America (video), January 27, 2021, https://www.youtube.com/watch?v=FfVx5jeh4Ic&t=1s (accessed July 25, 2022).

1. Table Bildung, "Wir haben Akquisitionen in der Pipeline," April 14, 2022, https://table.media/bildung/analyse/gostudent-nachhilfe-start-up/ (accessed November 6, 2022).

2. Mi Diao, Hui Kong, and Jinhua Zhao, "Impacts of Transportation Network Companies on Urban Mobility," *Nature Sustainability* 4 (2021): 494–500.

3. Eric Dawson, Sonya Passi, Sascha Haselmayer, and Karen Bannan (host), *The Commons Live!* presents "Taking the Slow Lane: Why Technology Isn't the Only Answer," New America (video), January 27, 2021, https://www .youtube.com/watch?v=FfVx5jeh4Ic&t=1s (accessed July 25, 2022).

4. Serlo, "Transparenz," https://de.serlo.org/transparenz (accessed November 6, 2022).

5. Eric Dawson, Sonya Passi, Sascha Haselmayer, and Karen Bannan (host), *The Commons Live!* presents "Taking the Slow Lane: Why Technology Isn't the Only Answer," New America (video), January 27, 2021, https://www .youtube.com/watch?v=FfVx5jeh4Ic&t=1s (accessed July 25, 2022).

6. Oliver Balch, "Making the Edit: Why We Need More Women in Wikipedia," *The Guardian*, November 29, 2019, https://www.theguardian .com/careers/2019/nov/28/making-the-edit-why-we-need-more-women-in -wikipedia (accessed November 6, 2022).

7. Eric Dawson, Sonya Passi, Sascha Haselmayer, and Karen Bannan (host), *The Commons Live!* presents "Taking the Slow Lane: Why Technology Isn't the Only Answer," New America (video), January 27, 2021, https://www .youtube.com/watch?v=FfVx5jeh4Ic&t=1s (accessed July 25, 2022).

8. University of New Mexico, "Project ECHO Bibliography," https://digital repository.unm.edu/hsc_echo_bibliography/ (accessed November 6, 2022).

9. Sascha Haselmayer, Jakob Rasmussen, and Aida Esteban, *Connected Cities: Your 256 Billion Euro Dividend* (London: Royal College of Art and Design, 2010).

CHAPTER 6

Epigraph: Taoiseach Leo Vardkar, "Speech by An Taoiseach, Following the Declaration on the Referendum on the Eighth Amendment," Department of the Taoiseach, Government of Ireland, May 27, 2018, https://www.gov.ie/en /speech/d7a266-speech-by-an-taoiseach-leo-varadkar-following-the-declaration -on-the/ (accessed January 8, 2023).

1. Raul Krauthausen, "Nicht ohne meinen Strohhalm!" *Spiegel Online*, September 24, 2021, https://www.spiegel.de/panorama/umweltschutz-und -behinderung-nicht-ohne-meinen-strohhalm-a-c9b45903-b174-4f52-befe -983de841ba45 (accessed November 6, 2022).

2. Universidad Católica Andrés Bello, "ENCOVI 2021: Condiciones de vida de los venezolanos: Entre emergencia humanitaria y pandemia," presentation, *Universidad Católica Andrés Bello*, September 2021, 48, https:// www.proyectoencovi.com/encovi-2021 (accessed November 6, 2022).

3. Stiven Tremaria, "Violent Caracas: Understanding Violence and Homicide in Contemporary Venezuela," *International Journal of Conflict and Violence* 10 (2016): 62, fig. 1.

4. Avery Trufelman (host), "Chandigarh: The Modernist Utopia," *Nice Try!* (podcast), June 6, 2019, https://open.spotify.com/episode/6qQRGybzYX FrJ9cbva32i3 (accessed November 6, 2022).

5. For the most comprehensive history of self-determination in Catuche, including the Tragedy of the Vargas, read Yohana Martín, *Catuche: Escuela de ciudadanía popular: Sistematización del proyecto de habilitación integral del barrio Catuche* (Caracas: abediciones, Universidad Católica Andrés Bello, 2019).

6. UNDP, "Human Development Reports: Venezuela," *Human Development Reports* (online), https://hdr.undp.org/data-center/specific-country-data#/countries/VEN (accessed November 12, 2022).

7. Shannon Doocy, Kathleen Page, and Tamara Taraciuk Broner, *Venezuela's Humanitarian Emergency* (Human Rights Watch, April 2019).

8. Álvaro Fuente, "Las madres que pusieron paz en la ciudad más violenta del mundo," *El País*, January 17, 2018.

9. CCS450, "El Sueño de Catuche," *Fundacion Espacio* (website), https://www.ccscity450.com/intervenciones_comun/el-sueno-de-catuche/# (accessed July 19, 2022).

10. Kristen Munson, "Living in a Food Desert in the Desert," *Utah Public Radio*, June 7, 2016, https://www.upr.org/news/2016-06-07/living-in-a-food-desert-in-the-desert (accessed November 6, 2022).

11. Navajo Epidemiology Center, "Healthy Diné Nation Act" (collection of articles), https://nec.navajo-nsn.gov/Projects/HDNA (accessed November 6, 2022).

12. Del Yazzie, Kristen Tallis, Caleigh Curley, Priscilla R. Sanderson, Regina Eddie, Timothy K Behrens, et al., "The Navajo Nation Healthy Diné Nation Act: A Two Percent Tax on Foods of Minimal-to-No Nutritious Value, 2015–2019," *Preventing Chronic Disease* 17 (September 2020) [e100], https://www.cdc.gov/pcd/issues/2020/20_0038.htm (accessed January 8, 2023).

13. Lauren Aratani, "Record Number of Native American Women Elected to Congress," *The Guardian* (online), November 4, 2020, https://www.theguardian.com/us-news/2020/nov/04/native-american-women-elected-congress-record-number (accessed November 12, 2022).

14. Anna North, "How Abortion Became a Partisan Issue in America," *Vox*, April 10, 2019, https://www.vox.com/2019/4/10/18295513/abortion-2020-roe-joe-biden-democrats-republicans (accessed November 6, 2022).

15. *Dobbs v. Jackson Women's Health Organization*, 597 U.S. (2022).

16. Elizabeth Sepper and Simon Scott (host), "New Texas Trigger Law Makes Abortion a Felony," NPR Weekend Edition Saturday, August 22, 2022, https://www.npr.org/2022/08/27/1119795665/new-texas-trigger-law-makes-abortion-a-felony (accessed January 8, 2023).

CHAPTER 7

Epigraph: Pema Chödrön, *When Things Fall Apart* (Boulder, CO: Shambhala Publications, 1997), 49.

1. These numbers are from the United Nations Volunteers (UNV) program, *2022 State of the World's Volunteerism Report: Building Equal and Inclusive Societies* (Bonn: United Nations Volunteers, 2021), 37–40.

2. GLS Bank and Karuna e.V. "Goldener Raum," https://www .goldenerraum.de/ (accessed November 5, 2022).

3. GEM (Global Entrepreneurship Monitor), *Global Entrepreneurship Monitor 2021/2022 Global Report: Opportunity Amid Disruption* (London: GEM, 2022).

CONCLUSION

Epigraph: Joan C. Tronto, *Who Cares?* (Ithaca, NY: Cornell Selects, 2015).

Acknowledgments

This book is for Julia, Sofía, Olivia, Currito, and Mochi. You made this book possible by being honest, inspiring me, challenging me, and giving me the space to write.

I want to express my special thanks to two people. Jim Anderson has been an incredible friend and mentor to me for years, and without his support and trust this book would not have been possible. Jan Weetjens has been my coach, helping me discover that you cannot ask someone their favorite color if you will only accept blue as an answer. If you know Jan, you will spot his wisdom in countless paragraphs.

It has been a special privilege to work with my editor Steve Piersanti and the entire wonderful team at Berrett-Koehler Publishing, as well as Dante Popple, Peggy Holman, and Zaid Hassan, who provided invaluable feedback as reviewers of the manuscript.

I want to thank all the people featured in these stories who were generous to take time out of their busy Slow Lane lives: Mark Johnson, Albina Ruiz, Yuraima Martín, César Martín, the late Father José Virtuoso (Joseito), Doris Barrento, Paul Cummins, Peter Moore, Denisa Livingston, Katherine Zappone, Professor Jane Suiter, Dorica Dan, Rosanne Haggerty, Kassa

Belay, David Harrington, Sonya Passi, Simon Köhl, Eric
Dawson, Dr. Sanjeev Arora, and Elisabeth Harsanji.

I also want to thank Hana Schank, Cecilia Muñoz, and
Karen Bannan for helping me take the path of writing this
book as we planned my Fellowship at New America. Leigh
O'Neil and Stacey Warady Gillett at Bloomberg Philanthropies
helped make it all possible. My dear friend Anthony Townsend
cheered me on and told me what it takes to write a book in the
first place. My Ashoka colleagues have been incredibly sup-
portive over the past few months: Laura Haverkamp, Katharina
Hinze, Judit Costa, Oda Heister, Odin Mühlenbein, Milena
Leszkowics-Weizman, Olga Shirobokova, Maria Zapata, Irina
Snissar, Diana Wells, and Manmeet Mehta. Thank you, too, for
helping me find stories and providing encouragement: Jeroo
Bellimoria, Astrid Mania, Christopher Swope, Charles Landry,
Robyn Bennett, Karen Harrison, and my dear friends David
Lubell, Gunnar Knechtel, and Hae-won Shin.

Finally, for many early and late seeds of inspiration, thank
you to Sanjay Purohit, Catherine du Toit, Peter Thomas, Marco
Steinberg, Chelsea Mauldin, Andrea Cooper, Stéphane Vincent,
James Oriel, Giulio Quaggiotto, Jason Pearman, Alex Ryan,
Christian Bason, James Oriel, Jesper Christiansen, Dominic
Campbell, Marc Winkelmann, and Jorge Fiori.

Index

About the Author

Thirty years ago, Sascha Haselmayer found his real passion as an architecture student when he visited Soweto, a township in South Africa, shortly after Nelson Mandela was elected president: to help enable the collective effort of people, community organizations, businesses, and governments to achieve real change.

Architecture, he realized, was not the tool for change he envisioned. But the skills of planning, designing, and problem-solving with communities proved invaluable as he set out to find out how best to enable this collaboration. And so, he became a serial social entrepreneur, building organizations to help cities become more collaborative in meeting their challenges and creating better futures.

Initially Sascha helped leaders in government, business, and universities reimagine cities as more inclusive places for the science-based innovation economy by helping to develop innovation districts in dozens of cities, throughout Europe and Asia. Advising leaders on the intersection of government policy, community development, and a rapidly changing economy brought him to co-initiate a global network of living laboratories in 2003, to put these collaborations to specific use and service to citizens. These labs proved highly effective at producing solutions that work.

But Sascha and his team uncovered a deeper problem, one that was holding back real change: city procurement, the $6 trillion a year business that has a big impact on the quality of public services that shape the world around us, such as education, social care, transport, climate, safety, and economic opportunity. Despite its size, public procurement was never intended to surface and reward the most meaningful solutions. Instead, it replicated old patterns and behaviors that held back progress on tackling our most urgent challenges.

In 2008, Sascha and his team applied the workings of architecture design competitions to public procurement more broadly, going on to found Citymart, an organization that by 2020 had helped 135 global cities adopt this new method and was replicated by countless organizations. Over the course of a decade, Sascha had been the leading advocate to reimagine what was considered a stale bureaucratic function into a creative public service.

Sascha's experience in Soweto, as well as countless other engagements in more than 150 cities around the world, didn't just spark his entrepreneurial journey. Having grown up in a firmly Fast Lane environment in Germany, working in these places and alongside their social innovators, Sascha encountered an alternative. That alternative grew in urgency as he began to experience the limitations of his own Fast Lane leadership as a social entrepreneur and a parent. A Fellowship at New America in 2020–21 helped him connect the dots with clarity, laying the foundation for this book. In late 2021, Sascha joined Ashoka Innovators for the Public, a global NGO where he helps make Ashoka's vision of creating an "Everyone a Changemaker" world a reality, by changing mind-sets and empowering more people to contribute to real change.

Along the way, Sascha has taken his message around the world by lecturing at universities such as the London School of Economics and the University of Chicago; by being a trusted adviser to philanthropies and think tanks such as the Rockefeller Foundation, Bloomberg Philanthropies, and the Aspen Institute; and by advising governments and public institutions like the government of South Africa, the World Bank Group, and the Nordic Council of Ministers. His work has been profiled by global media, including the *New York Times*. In 2011 he was awarded the prestigious Ashoka Fellowship.

Sascha has two daughters and lives in Berlin with his wife, Julia. You can visit his website at saschahaselmayer.com.

Berrett–Koehler
Publishers

Berrett-Koehler is an independent publisher dedicated to an ambitious mission: *Connecting people and ideas to create a world that works for all.*

Our publications span many formats, including print, digital, audio, and video. We also offer online resources, training, and gatherings. And we will continue expanding our products and services to advance our mission.

We believe that the solutions to the world's problems will come from all of us, working at all levels: in our society, in our organizations, and in our own lives. Our publications and resources offer pathways to creating a more just, equitable, and sustainable society. They help people make their organizations more humane, democratic, diverse, and effective (and we don't think there's any contradiction there). And they guide people in creating positive change in their own lives and aligning their personal practices with their aspirations for a better world.

And we strive to practice what we preach through what we call "The BK Way." At the core of this approach is *stewardship,* a deep sense of responsibility to administer the company for the benefit of all of our stakeholder groups, including authors, customers, employees, investors, service providers, sales partners, and the communities and environment around us. Everything we do is built around stewardship and our other core values of *quality, partnership, inclusion,* and *sustainability.*

This is why Berrett-Koehler is the first book publishing company to be both a B Corporation (a rigorous certification) and a benefit corporation (a for-profit legal status), which together require us to adhere to the highest standards for corporate, social, and environmental performance. And it is why we have instituted many pioneering practices (which you can learn about at www.bkconnection.com), including the Berrett-Koehler Constitution, the Bill of Rights and Responsibilities for BK Authors, and our unique Author Days.

We are grateful to our readers, authors, and other friends who are supporting our mission. We ask you to share with us examples of how BK publications and resources are making a difference in your lives, organizations, and communities at www.bkconnection.com/impact.

Dear reader,

Thank you for picking up this book and welcome to the worldwide BK community! You're joining a special group of people who have come together to create positive change in their lives, organizations, and communities.

What's BK all about?

Our mission is to connect people and ideas to create a world that works for all.

Why? Our communities, organizations, and lives get bogged down by old paradigms of self-interest, exclusion, hierarchy, and privilege. But we believe that can change. That's why we seek the leading experts on these challenges—and share their actionable ideas with you.

A welcome gift

To help you get started, we'd like to offer you a **free copy** of one of our bestselling ebooks:

www.bkconnection.com/welcome

When you claim your **free ebook**, you'll also be subscribed to our blog.

Our freshest insights

Access the best new tools and ideas for leaders at all levels on our blog at ideas.bkconnection.com.

Sincerely,

Your friends at Berrett-Koehler

MIX
Paper from responsible sources
FSC® C016245

Certified
Corporation